BLUE HEAVEN

I want to thank God for trivial things, the ones that get me up in the morning. I look through the papers but the news is so heavy. They are throwing bricks and bottles in Northern Ireland and no politician has a nice word to say for another in public, which is a pity as privately they are probably old pals. Anyway, I can't take it. Why don't they give us some cheerful news instead? I would willingly pay a penny more for news which helps to get me up. Hasn't someone been dealt a complete suit in bridge? That's what I'd like to read! Or that someone has sussed out a way to prop up a soufflé and keep it up. Such things are equally real and just as significant.

**Also by the same author,
and available from Coronet:**

Bolts from the Blue

About the Author

Rabbi Lionel Blue spent his childhood in the
East End of London. Known to many for his
work in both Jewish and Christian circles – he
lectures in comparative religion, conducts
Jewish–Christian retreats and is Convenor of
an ecclesiastical court – he is known to many
more through his broadcasts on Radio 4's
Today programme and his many books, among
them KITCHEN BLUES and BOLTS FROM
THE BLUE. He is cook to the Catholic press
(*The Universe*) and with Rabbi Dr Jonathan
Magonet edits the revision of the Reform
Jewish liturgy.

Blue Heaven

Rabbi Lionel Blue

CORONET BOOKS
Hodder and Stoughton

Illustrated by
Albert Rusling

Copyright © 1987 by Rabbi
Lionel Blue

First published in Great Britain
in 1987 by Hodder and
Stoughton Limited

Coronet Edition 1988

**British Library Cataloguing
in Publication Data**

Blue, Lionel
Blue heaven.
I. Title
828'.91402
ISBN 0-340-48905-7

Printed and bound in Great Britain
for Hodder and Stoughton
Paperbacks, a division of Hodder
and Stoughton Ltd., Mill Road,
Dunton Green, Sevenoaks, Kent
TN13 2YA (Editorial Office: 47
Bedford Square London WC1B
3DP) by Richard Clay Ltd.,
Bungay, Suffolk.

To James Cummings, who helped me prepare
this manuscript

Contents

Thank You

I thank the many creatures, human and animal, who have enriched my religion and experience – church people and charwomen, Jewish story tellers, a three legged dog, merry nuns, Yiddisher mommas and many gentle gentiles. I've been blessed with good friends and am grateful to Phyllis Moss, Alec Hekford and William Wightman for putting up with me for many years.

I thank my mother and aunt for their memories, typing and tenderness; the staff of the *Today* programme, and 'Thought for the Day' for their genial good nature, so early in the morning; and the people I came to know through *The Standard* and *The Universe*. It has been a pleasure to broadcast, write and cook for them, and I share some of that pleasure in these writings – may they be for a blessing!

Introduction

When I first caught religion at university (you catch it from other people like measles) I tried very hard to break through the barrier which separates human beings from God. At services I screwed up my eyes and gazed and gazed at eternal lights and candles, lusting after voices and visions. I did see things, of course – I saw spots and stars, but didn't know how to divine their meaning.

Walking in the street, I tried to shut out the silly, secular world around me, with its rows and rumpus, and concentrate on eternity instead. I nearly got there quicker than I bargained for, because I bumped into a bus. The driver jeered, I turned sulky, and words passed between us which contemplatives shouldn't contemplate.

I wanted some special revelation to fall from heaven and hit me, bonk! on the head in the high street. My life would then be bathed in blessings, obvious to any discerning believer, and who knows, they might even sniff the odour of my sanctity. (I was adolescent and fascinated by contemplative kitsch.)

Well, it was fun while it lasted, though it didn't last long, because real holiness doesn't happen that way. The real knowledge of God didn't fall on me from above, it seeped up from below. Bits of it came to me, for example while I was cooking cabbage in a kitchen, and a moment of understanding while I was riding a bad-tempered camel on a Costa package holiday. It came to me mediated by dogs, beggars, camels (as I've just said), colleagues, friends, foes, and through my mother and aunt and memories of their mother – may she rest in peace!

Faith was funnier than I had expected, and to be honest, religion more real than I really wanted.

These stories will tell you what happened.

A Suburban Sanctuary

When I first read the gospels, I was moved by the cry of pain from their pages when 'the Son of Man' says he has 'nowhere to lay his head' though the foxes have holes and the birds have nests.

Jews are a wandering people. They have had to change their country and culture 'more often than their shoes'. They therefore have an intense feeling for home.

Mine is an ordinary semi in a suburb in England, but my elderly mother and aunt share it, and so does the memory of their mother and the shade of a dog we all loved, who bossed us about.

It is not a *'machine à habiter'* but a sanctuary, where the pieties are partly kept and parties are planned, where friends become family, where sentimental rubbish is treated with reverence and where more prayers (and imprecations) are said than in a synagogue.

Tempted to trust

Four years ago I set up home with my elderly mother and her older sister. They inhabit the ground floor, I perch on the first and we get on better than I expected. Our rows haven't been resolved but they've run out of steam. I'm grateful because we've found each other again – in time!

Some months ago my mother went into hospital and I flapped around trying to arrange transport for my aunt to visit her. 'You're worrying too much,' said my mother unconcernedly, lying back in bed and eyeing the doctor. 'I've got everything I need,' and she hopefully dabbed on more perfume from a big bottle of Charlie.

My aunt thanked me prettily. 'Don't go to all that trouble, Lionel,' she said, and then had an inspiration. 'I'll send her a nice postcard instead!'

Now, my mother and aunt have stood by each other facing death, the dole, bombs, miscarriages and two world wars. Their love is real, not romantic, and as my mother said tartly to me, 'Don't make us play pious games, Lionel! We're too old.'

When she came home our reunited family sat cosily in the kitchen, chewing over a platter of chops and the papers. My mother perused the financial forecasts, because she finds them funny.

I looked at them both and realised that age was not the demon I had dreaded when I was an adolescent –

when I stood in front of mirrors examining my hair for fall-out. I should have been more trusting, for age had liberated us from expectation, each other's and our own. We could at last be honest with each other and with ourselves. For the first time I felt like blessing God who makes us age.

And since age contained so much surprise perhaps death, which lay waiting for all three of us just over the horizon, might surprise us too, and dazzle us despite the pain. Perhaps I would meet that inner voice, my counsellor for thirty years. Perhaps not, I thought. My voice might turn out to be a trick of my imagination.

'The world's cheated you,' said my voice, responding to my thoughts as it always does, 'and above all you've cheated yourself. But I've never cheated you.'

I rapidly ran over the years gone by. No, it never had.

'I've been there whenever you've wanted me,' said the voice, 'and sometimes when you haven't,' it added as an afterthought.

'You'll be there at my death,' I said urgently, ignoring the innuendo, 'I'll hold you to that.'

'I always hold you. Don't you know that by now?' it said flatly.

Another voice suddenly crashed into our conversation, its thoughts in curious counterpoint to mine. 'Lionel,' said my mother, peering over her paper, 'if the rich paid the poor to die for them there'd be no unemployment.'

I choked on a chop. No mystic moment could survive that. But for a long time after, I felt light and loving. I trusted and it showed.

Dear child

Last Wednesday, when I got home from Birmingham, my mother and my aunt pressed into my hands their birthday presents, for at midnight I would be fifty-six-years-old to me, and fifty-six-years-young to them.

There was some chocolate cake my aunt had baked, a ten-pound note put aside from their pension and a packet of photos they gave me diffidently because they weren't sure I would want them.

So to reassure them, I sat beside them on the sofa, munching the chocolate cake, and together we turned over the yellowing pictures.

There was my mother and her sisters in beach pyjamas, strutting out arm in arm, three smart girls who had saved to go to Margate and got there. There was their mother peering nervously into the camera some sunny evening in Stepney long ago. There was my mother again, proud possessor of a dead fox slung around her neck, with limp legs and nasty glass eyes – very thirties, very smart. And there was my youngest aunt, her sister, fresh and round-faced, lurching along

on Louis heels because she wanted to be a femme fatale, though God has designed her otherwise. And then there was me, a child looking speculatively out of the picture, curious as to what kind of life lay beyond the frame.

I hadn't noticed that child for years. I'd never considered him or thought of him. But now I suddenly wanted to speak to him as if there were some unfinished business between us.

So after my mother and aunt kissed me and went to bed, I sat on, sucking a pencil, laboriously composing a letter just as I used to long ago.

Dear child [I wrote],

I don't know how we are related, if we are, for not one cell of your body lives in mine. I know you tried to imagine me once or twice as you gazed into the future, but you wouldn't recognise me now. I don't know if I've been your friend or foe, for there was a lot of niceness in you I never allowed to grow, but I didn't have much choice!

It is of course your birthday too, and I remember the presents you longed for – a cup cake at the Corner House, meeting a millionaire who would give dad a job.

But I cannot reach through the glass that separates us and can give you nothing.

I can't even pass on some knowledge which would make your life easier. That sort of knowledge, as you'll learn later, always comes too late, after events not before them.

But as I look at you, your image gazes into me and I see myself without the rucksack of anger and reproaches I've got used to carrying on my back. I wonder what it would be like to let it go. I know from your face that it wasn't always there. Perhaps I can, because as I get older I am closer to being a child again, a second time round, and I become free from grown-up hopes and fears. They say that when people remonstrated with old Golda Meir for smoking, she just said, 'What should happen to me? I should die young.' Well, there are lots of things I've stopped worrying about too – there isn't time.

But her wisecrack has broken my mood and I can't continue this letter – it is too personal. But from it comes this advice for all of you who read it – present or past.

When you try to reconcile yourself to God and to love your neighbours, spare some love for the child who lives within you – whom you haven't thought about for years. He too has a present to give you, though you can give him nothing in return.

Oh, to be in England!

I have fallen in love with England, a land I scarcely know, like most Londoners. ('The jungle begins at Watford,' they tell you from Tottenham to Tooting.) And what is England? I first began to know it when I was abroad. I walked through the streets of Haifa and longed for lines of Victorian houses under slanting rain with water everywhere, oozing up from the damp course and dripping down from bay windows. In Cannes I craved brown and bottled sauce and English mustard. Rome was an oasis! I was given tea by an English nun. We ate cress and cucumber sandwiches and iced fancies and felt like furtive children having a treat amongst all that baroquerie-rococorie.

How attractive despised English food is when you're abroad! They serve you 'médaillons' of this or 'minceur' of that, when all you want is marmite on toast and another jug of hot water, miss!

And England means cardboard notices at country crossroads, telling you to patronise the bazaar at St Something to prop up their perpendicular church tower which is tottering. It's been around a long time it's true, but not much longer, if the notice is to be believed. Unless, that is, you invest in a bottle of home made chutney, or guess the number of currants in a canary-yellow cake. On such frail foundations our heritage rests. To prop it up, we must make sacrifices and pander to our paunch.

And England means the seaside with retired couples sitting in cars, tightly sealed against any air or ozone, gazing happily and emptily at the smooth sea and munching pasties and peppermints. If they did their thing in the Himalayas, where emptiness is appreciated, they would be greeted as great gurus.

And there's the modern takeaway England of curry and chips, and Chinese chop-suey with mushy peas, served by slant-eyed orientals speaking scouse – Everton or Liverpool supporters to a man. It's an entrancing mixture, if people are prepared to enjoy it before they emote and demonstrate and deride it. Our country is a sort of casserole, in which communities are cooking together. Let's hope we've got the right recipe. The ingredients are fine if treated fairly.

And then there is a holy England, beneath the skin of the secular one if you have 'ears to hear and eyes to see'. I wandered into Lichfield and wondered why George Fox had walked through it feeling he was deep in the blood of martyrs and crying, 'Woe to the bloody city of

Lichfield!' It seems a strange statement amongst all that gentility. And I'd like to go to King's Lynn too, and see if there are any relics or remnants of Margery Kempe around, that garrulous medieval tomb-trotter who should be the patron saint of Awaydays and the Tourist Board.

And then there are those curiosities only the English can appreciate. The BR fare tariffs for example, curious, complex and constantly changing, to keep us on the hop and mentally alert. There are the coded communications in the English class war, which can only be comprehended this side of the channel. 'What is she trying to say?' said a puzzled continental friend one morning, as an old lady I knew hissed at us in a yacht club, 'NQOCD.' I pondered this murky message and had a moment of inspiration of which I was proud.

'She is referring to that other nice elderly lady at the next table,' I said succinctly, 'and she is telling us that she is "Not Quite Our Class Dear".' How much more interesting than that silly old SPQR you see written all over so many ruins in Rome.

'Oh, land of tottering church towers, toasted teacakes, class and crumpets, I love you.'

My paranoid pooch

I sat on a park bench near the dog cemetery opposite Lancaster Gate Station and thought about clever and classy dogs. Though the cemetery was firmly locked, I had peered through the railings and read fragments from the tombstones. It was a mausoleum of upper-crust canines, all of them noted when alive for their fidelity, integrity, intelligence and looks. They had the lot.

And I began to think of my poor pooch Re'ach, who had died not far away at the age of eighteen and who had none of those qualities in any abundance. She was a big-boned bitch, a mongrel mixture of Labrador, Alsatian and other oddments. She was very large and rather loony, because she thought she was a lap dog but she wasn't built that way. Nor was she intelligent or ingenious or brave. If any burglar had the sense to bring along dog 'chocs', she was his – for the duration of the 'choc' drops, that is.

She knew where the drops were kept, of course, in a plastic box with a lid, on top of her toys. But she never learned about lids. She just howled piteously beside it, until some weakling bribed her to stop.

She was also quite paranoid. If there was a bang from an exhaust she was away like a rabbit, not a dog, seeking sanctuary under my bed, where she stayed till the end of hostilities. She was convinced till her dying day that 'they' were all gunning for her, Re'ach, as if they had nothing better to do with their time. (Did she learn it from me?)

She was no brave bonzo, as I have said. Despite her big body, she was girlish and terrified of mice, though the way she dealt with any particular mouse was novel, but ill considered and quite mad. When she saw one, she rushed into a corner and poked her head into it, closing her eyes tight shut, presenting her great trembling back to the very mild mouse, who seemed quite fond of her. The logic of the situation was clear. If she couldn't see him, then he couldn't see her, and *voilà* (I interpret for her, of course), that was all there was to it.

I have known many more intelligent dogs of far better character. I knew a lovely one in Malta called Honey. She was the only dog I've ever met who could smile – most dogs look clerically grave. But if you called out 'Honey', then she would curl back her lip and expose her molars in a fearsome grin. I had never seen a dog curl its lips before, and the result was unnerving but very clever.

The most intelligent dog I have ever met had only three legs. Someone must have kicked him as a puppy in a Mediterranean village. This had dislocated his hip and rheumatism had set in. His name was Mac and he lived among the garbage dumps. Though wary of humans, quite sensibly because they can be very nasty animals indeed, he was judicious about them. Selectively, with sense and discrimination, he made friends and acquaintances among them, though without illusion.

But to return to Re'ach, every part of the park reminded me of her. Once she tried to chase a duck, but the bird had turned and Re'ach had fled insanely across the green and jumped into my lap, all wet and sticky, reminding me with woofs and trembling that I was her protector.

Another time, while looking for some sunken stick, she spied a stockbroker type, pointing out with a rolled umbrella some distant spire to his Sloane Square girl-friend. This umbrella Re'ach quite wrongly regarded as her original stick, now renewed and restored. It was impossible to shake her conviction of ownership for she could only keep one idea at a time in her tiny but tenacious mind. There was a tussle, a tirade of blistering oaths and barks, and two black paw marks appeared on the stockbroker's silk shirt. I tried to disarm Re'ach with the same intensity with which she had tried to own the brolly. It did neither of us any good.

It's really a wonder she wasn't assassinated, but at eighteen-years-old she died peacefully in Bayswater, near her beloved park, with her head in my lap. I didn't get her a memorial stone but I made a gift to an animal charity in her name. Perhaps 'charity redeems from death' works for dogs as well as for humans. I hope so, because heaven for me will always encompass an early autumn morning in a park with reddening leaves and bright blue sky, and a big black dog.

Room service

When I leave London people ask me to come and stay with them. The invitations are light-hearted but I am scared of accepting. Every house has its own rules, assumed by the family but an obstacle course for the stranger.

Can you pull the chain in the middle of the night? It's vulgar, but vital. Will it unleash a roaring Niagara, loud enough to wake both the quick and the dead asleep? It doesn't seem couth to question your hosts on their plumbing. (They might get embarrassing about yours.)

And what is acceptable morning dress in the provinces? Can you be bright and breezy in pyjama bottoms, or is it dressy stuff in brogues and hacking jackets? I once selected the latter and found the family scoffing saté in sarongs – they had just holidayed in Indonesia.

And what do you talk about? Do you guzzle in gloom or be bright like my mother, who consumes steak and chips spiced with gossip and tomato sauce? Personally I prefer to read theology in silence at breakfast – I got used to it in monasteries. But it may seem odd, I grant you, if your guest just grunts at you as he moodily munches his muesli, peering over the *Confessions of St Augustine*.

Another problem is who can you complain to if anything goes wrong? What can you say if your electric razor bursts into a sheet of flame as you are tidying up your neckline? Or if the punch provided the previous night leaves you still pickled, muddled and befuddled the following morning? You can hardly raise hell with your hosts, so you had better be grumpy with God. (Don't worry, He's used to it!)

Because of all these booby traps, I head for hotels be they ne'er so humble. At least you can moan at the manager, and if they are not as humble as all that, the gadgetry is gorgeous. I programme alarm calls I haven't got the electronic know-how to cancel, and bounce on the bed, a childhood delight which has never palled and which I daren't do in a dwelling.

In recent years I have noticed that everything in hotels is growing bigger – rather like the experience of Alice down the rabbit hole. Single beds have become doubles, and doubles have developed into well-sprung tennis courts, available for other games and goings on. As I sprawl and dream diagonally, not straight up and down as I should, this suits me fine.

But unexpectedly these great modern hotels have given me a spiritual plus. I am a worldly person, who has tried for years to be detached and other-worldly. I have moaned in monasteries and gone after gurus to get this experience which my teachers tell me is a mystical must. I get nearest to it when I am perched in a private

27

and impersonal pad on the fifteenth floor of a hotel block, lost and lonely amid the luxury. I am insulated against the world and feel nowhere. It's a necessity as well as a pleasure to pray in such a place – and it's on the house!

The Basics of Belief

Apart from professional theologians who are paid to puzzle over definitions and dogmas, most people keep well away from them, because some seem dated, some difficult, and some quite dreadful – in the old sense.

Many turn instead to religious experience which seems refreshing, simple and sensuous, but it is no substitute for the hard stuff.

The basics of belief have to be sorted out, and a cemetery is a gentle place to do it. Sitting on a bench, you can consider death, doom, sin, salvation – the lot. When you work out what they mean to you personally, they lose some of their strangeness and a lot of their terror. If you treat them with respect but without idolatry you begin to know where you stand – which makes life a lot less confusing in this world and the next.

Strewth!

'Lord,' I said this morning as I was shaving, 'what's all this about hell?'

For a moment He said nothing, but He's quite perceptive really, so He continued, casual like, 'Anything bothering you, Lionel? What's up?' And, of course, He was right. I was upset because I had got talking to a man who seemed so nice at first that I gave him a coin for his cause. He then explained to me that he wanted to warn me about hell. I'd heard that one before and smiled. But I couldn't stop his explanations. He was single-minded and serious, and step by ghastly step he demonstrated my danger to me.

I didn't follow it all, but somewhere in the cosmos there was a vast concentration camp. God was the commandant of this hell and His angels supplied the tortures and the gas. Unlike the Third Reich, it wouldn't last for a thousand years but for ever. I would go to it, he said, and all my family. My poor old mother and aunt hadn't endured enough in this world, apparently. God would have it in for them in the next as well.

I was annoyed with the man, and more annoyed with me, because he scared me stiff in spite of myself. Being a wobbler I am always impressed by strongminded people. And even if God forgives my sins, I never find it easy to forgive myself.

SAVE
OUR
VICAR
FUND

'Well, is there a hell?' I asked God apprehensively,
waving my razor upwards.

'What did they teach you in the seminary?' He said.

'Well, the rabbis discussed it one and a half thousand
years ago.'

'And what did they decide?' He seemed interested.

'They decided it didn't exist – but only by a majority
vote.'

'Anything more?' He asked quite curiously.

'Some said, though they were in a minority, that we
were already in hell. This world was it!'

'Well, some are certainly,' He said sadly. 'Which reminds me, Lionel. Instead of worrying about hell so
much, I want you to work at it a bit more. There's that
poor old chap who says he's got AIDS. If you rang him
up and did his shopping and went round for a natter
and a cuppa, you might turn his hell into heaven this
morning.'

'But I'm neurotic about catching things,' I said. 'It might be heaven for him but it would be hell for me.'

'Don't be silly, of course it won't,' said God. 'If you visit him, you know jolly well I'll visit you, and if I'm present how can it be hell? Really?' He sounded rather miffed.

'Can I really change hell into heaven?' I said hastily, trying to be tactful and shift the conversation.

'I don't see why not,' He answered mollified. 'After all, they're both inside you.

'By the way,' He added hesitantly, 'forgive Me for asking, Lionel, but why did your acquaintance say I created this cosmic concentration camp?'

'Out of love,' I said, dead pan, 'because You liked the inmates so much?'

'Strewth!' God said – a word I have never ever heard Him use, either before or since.

Another way of living

Suddenly I had a free afternoon, a committee was cancelled and I was freed and released from my clerical cage.

Normally I would go and visit my friend. She would say, 'My dear, you do look distraught,' and then she would sit me down in her shabby armchair and pour me tea from a silver teapot with its strainer and slop basin and give me a toasted teacake. And while I talked she would listen, giving me her whole attention, not just scraps, which is all most people have to offer. She was truly a gentlewoman, and gentile too, which had been hard for us both.

We first met at a college ball in Oxford – she in her best and only ball-gown, me in a utility dinner-jacket. We had been debonair and danced the Charleston round the ballroom. One, two, three, kick, one, two, three, kick. It was a fascinating dance, she said. I found out years later that she lay in bed for a week afterwards with bruised shins, bruised fortunately not broken, and her only gown was now a housecoat.

She had died with the same courage and composure, worried about washing her smalls, and lest her dying might be a nuisance.

The sun was shining that afternoon. I bought a choc-ice and a bunch of flowers and I sat in the cemetery on a bench near her grave, wondering where she was now, who she was and even what she was. With my imagination I tried to speak with her, probing the great barrier of death to find a chink through which we could talk. Lots of bereaved people try it. But I gave up disgusted with myself. Even if something did sound in my mind, I would be the ventriloquist and her shade would be my dummy. It was both silly and sentimental. My friend would have thought it intrusive and vulgar and she was neither.

I was relieved when a voice broke in on my grief, for I found I was not the only mourner there. There was an old lady at the other end of the bench, whom I had been too absorbed to notice. Her cat had died, her beloved Thomas, the lone companion of her retirement in a small bedsit. She had buried him in the communal yard and put a stone over him, but his tomb needed a text and there seemed none suitable in scripture, for neither prophets nor apostles were partial to pets. I took out a pocket Bible and together we searched. I was not much help but I was willing to listen and for this she thanked me.

Thank my friend, I thought, for it was only from her

34

that I had learned to listen. Monologues are more my line for I am a self-centred person. We parted, but as I went sadly through the cemetery gates my heart suddenly leapt up. Though my friend hadn't spoken to me, her goodness had spoken through me and in me. It would stay with me in this life till we could meet again, as long as I was willing to be its home. It was enough. My visit to the cemetery had not been in vain.

Poor devil

She was a nice lady who lived in a cosy cottage and I congratulated her on it. 'I'm going to get rid of it,' she said sadly. 'A coven of devil worshippers meet near the compost heap at the bottom of my garden.' I glanced at her suspiciously, but she seemed a commonsense type. 'I suppose being a minister you often come across such things.'

'Well, I don't,' I said a few weeks later in a fellow clergyman's kitchen, as I chatted to his wife. She came from the continent and as her opinions were as strong as her coffee, I wondered what she thought of the haunted compost heap.

But the telephone interrupted us and I heard her answer evenly several times, 'Yes, of course I'll tell my husband. Yes, I assure you. No, I won't forget. Yes, I promise you.

'That woman will never believe me,' she said glumly, as she sat down and leafed through the morning papers. 'My husband is a marvellous minister, but he hasn't got time for everybody. So when they can't get through to him they say, "He's a lovely man who would love to listen to me all day long, but that foreign wife of his is

a jealous she-devil, who won't allow him near me, and I can't get through her to him – she's so cunning."' She sighed. 'I'm no good at committees or counselling, but people seem to like him more if they like me less, and since they can't do without their devils, I'll be one for his sake.'

'That's tough,' I said.

'I've had enough practice at it. I'm a bit Jew and a bit gypsy, and when I was a child in Eastern Europe, parents taught their children to make horns at me when I wanted to play with them. And then the war came and the Nazis shot the gypsies and sent the Jews to the camps, because they said devils like us shouldn't live alongside decent people like them.

'Lionel,' she burst out, 'tell your nice lady not to sell her cosy cottage. Only comic devils dance round rubbish heaps. The real ones dance in us, they're part of us though we don't acknowledge them.'

She ticked them off on her fingers. 'The deadly ones are: the anger we suppress, the hatred we hide, our desires which are too hot to handle, the bit of ourselves we don't love and punish in others.'

She pointed to the morning papers in disgust. 'In the Psalms, people had the guts to blame themselves or God. Now they blame all their problems on politicians, poor devils.

'Tell me a joke to make me less angry,' she said. 'Not a sad Jewish joke but a bright British one.'

'OK,' I said. 'Two ancient Britons went to a Bar Mitzvah and as they were dancing round a compost heap one said to the other in Yiddish, "Hymie . . ."'

'You devil,' she said, and smiled for the first time that morning. I hoped she looked a little less haunted.

The hard stuff

When the ferry turned turtle at Zeebrugge and nearly two hundred holidaymakers were drowned I couldn't find anything cheering or cheerful in me. I have travelled on that ferry too often, and know the harbour wall well. There's no point in avoiding them, so I shall try to deal with the hard questions the disaster left in its wake. Why does a good God let such disasters happen and if He does, why worship Him?

Like most people, I went into religion not for God's sake but for my own. I didn't get enough from this life, so I thought I'd get more in the next.

I discussed God with a girl in Benidorm. She wore the regulation outfit – bangle, bikini, beach ball and a nine-carat crucifix for good luck. But how could the image of a tortured, dying man bring good luck? I asked, puzzled. She pouted and went off to bounce her ball with a more cheerful chap.

The same question surfaced when a foreign friend took me to a meeting, for his country was on the verge of war. A venerable clergyman addressed us: 'God would never fail His people. Their capital could never be captured.'

Everyone clapped, including a general on the platform, but his eyes looked cynical. I must have looked cynical too, because with one of them he winked at me.

He was right. Belief in God is no guarantee against disaster. Greater and godlier cities had fallen – Rome, Jerusalem, Constantinople, Lhasa. I thought about the horrors of Jewish history. No divine hand had lifted the terrified from the trucks to the concentration camps.

When this message hits home, you either lose your faith or get converted to it properly. Conversion doesn't mean changing religious brand names, just accepting the implications of what you've got. Fortunately, I met a teacher who told me a tale from the hidden heart of Judaism – the Cabbalah.

'Before God created the Universe, He abandoned a part of Himself, to leave an emptiness in which we and the world could exist in freedom. In the emptiness are scattered sparks of His shattered divinity. It is our duty to redirect them back to God – to reassemble and to reunite Him, so to speak.'

My faith was turned inside out. I could no longer pray, 'God help me!' but, 'How can I help God?' for His only power over me was the love He inspired in me. And He wasn't above disaster, He suffered in it. He wasn't far, just too close for comfort. His sparks were in the man on the ferry who made himself into a human bridge, in the wheelchair granny who went to save a stranger, and in me too, pushing me to give pounds not pennies to the disaster fund.

A rabbi said to God, 'I don't want your heaven and I'm not scared of your hell. I only want You.' That's the real answer, though I'm not religious enough yet to cope with it.

Travellers' Tales

Some seekers find eternity inside themselves and save themselves a lot of trouble because they need go no further than their sitting room to understand the metaphysics of this world and the next. Mother Julian experienced both, walled up in her anchor-hold in a Norwich church with only one window which gave on to the world outside.

I admire her, but am more closely drawn to her contemporary, that muddled, middle-class, middle-aged mystic Margery Kempe, who endured all the horrors of medieval package-pilgrimages for the same end – the knowledge and the love of God.

Holidays expose the hidden workings of mind and soul because they are the point at which reality and fantasy meet. Travel takes me away from my built-in defences. Forlorn in foreign parts and unfamiliar hotels, holiness is the only home available. I have to match my outer journey with an inner one. Like poor Margery Kempe, I am more mystical on the move. My case is not so extreme of course, but spiritually speaking, tourism certainly turns me on.

A dream of marble halls

The most memorable holiday I ever had was also the cheapest. The brochure said I could have five or six nights and four days (or was it the other way round. I lost count of the nights and days – I was too confused) for about a tenner – everything thrown in. It was long, long ago! I have always had a weakness for bargains and I needed a break, so I signed on and joined the jolly package.

We were sent off in the early hours of the morning when the departure lounge lived up to its name and seemed reserved for the dear departed. It looked ghostly and we looked ghastly. I knew it would take me five or six days and four nights (or vice versa) to recover – and then, my God, I thought, it would all begin again. For the first time in my life I wrung my hands.

We arrived at our hotel in the early hours and its unexpected grandeur muddled me more than ever. The foyer was filled with marble and the chandeliers were like those in Lyons Corner Houses before the war. It was stupefying and I wondered if I had wandered on to a film set. There was even more marble in my room – so much marble that it reminded me of that superior suburban cemetery where I shall eventually lodge as a long-term guest (a synagogue kindly gave me free burial rights as a parting gift – it was well meant).

Before I tried to sleep I examined the furniture and

had another surprise – it was concreted in! Surely clientèle who were fit for such marble halls would not nick the commodes. Such low suspicions in such high living didn't fit.

There was a lot that didn't fit, in fact. Just as I dozed off, an institutional bell clanged along the classy corridors. Blearily, I went down to breakfast and in a dream ate sugared buns under crystal chandeliers at a table with two elderly ladies and one drunk.

The ladies said the weather wasn't what they had expected in the south. I said politely it would be more bloody in the north, and the drunk reproved me in a hoarse whisper for using foul language in front of the fair sex. He told me to mind my q's and p's. P's and q's, I corrected absentmindedly, and ill advisedly. An explosion was averted by an announcement. Shortly after breakfast we would be welcome in the local nightclub whose management would treat us to one free glass of 'champagne' each. The ladies gasped. They had never been near a night-club, nor had I, at noon.

In the club itself some grey light glimmered through the cracks on to the purple poufs and scarlet tables. I sipped the sweet froth and decided I had fallen down a rabbit hole and would make the best of it.

The only other hole open in town, where we could also make the best of it, was a liqueur shop (not a liquor shop). It sold every liqueur imaginable and some which weren't. At 11 a.m. you could freak out on sweet alcohol, flavoured with banana, quince, quinine or gold-leaf. Some looked like perfume and some just tasted like it. The weather was appalling and the town deserted. We looked at each other and had another one for the road – though if I remember rightly, none of the roads there were complete.

When we got back to the hotel we were told to tone up for a pageant of local dance. Then we would visit a

44

shrine, and then we would begin some bingo. Never was so much experienced by so few for so little.

Since that package so many years ago, my admiration for the value provided by our tourist industry for the British holidaymaker has never wavered. The latter didn't want to let the side (what side?) down. So they queued for their morning bubbly, and prayed at the shrine, and pretended to be partial to fancy dress and sugared buns instead of rashers, and when they were holed up in the hotel by a gale they sang 'Lily of Laguna' and 'We'll hang out the washing on the Siegfried Line' – which startled a German group who were being loaded in just as we were packed out.

Since those far-off days, costs have become keener on the costas and you don't get much marble now for a tenner, if any. But the breakfast buns still carry the same quota of sugar. I can't remember where I went. Come to think of it, I never knew.

Senile delinquent

On the crowded bus I offered my seat to a senior citizen. 'Keep it yourself, Grandad,' he said nastily. He then wriggled as far down the bus as he could get while the rest of the passengers tittered. Occasionally he threw me a malevolent look. Because your world grows old with you, you notice the passing of time in strangers but not in yourself or your friends.

But time had passed, and I was reminded of it when I rang up to make enquiries about sheltered accommodation for an elderly friend. 'How old is he?' said the lady at the other end. 'Over eighty, but very fit,' I replied. 'Oh dear,' she said, 'that's far too late. You have to come into the scheme much earlier.' 'What, seventy?' I asked. 'Well,' she answered apologetically, 'perhaps a little earlier than that.' 'Sixty?' I said stiffly. 'Yes,' she said, 'that would be about right, but don't leave it too late.' 'You mean,' I said icily, 'I should not be applying for my friend but for myself.' 'How old are you?' she asked briskly. 'Fifty-seven,' I replied sulkily. 'Just right!' she said, 'I'll send you a form,' and she rang off hurriedly.

It rankled! So I signed on for a holiday where I could learn to be my age and snooze with fellow seniles. But it wasn't like that. Our hotel and hostesses were lovely. Nothing was too much trouble, whether it was TV, tea, or transport by air, coach or camel. One day we had culture in chilly churches and on the next we trotted on a conga line through a casbah, where we feasted on a combination of herb tea and couscous with a belly dancer who wore combinations, of the woolly sort I thought, and a fender round her front like a jeep.

At lunch and dinner we were given our bottles, like the ones we had as babies, but with stronger stuff inside, of course – no teats and the same effect. They certainly sedated me into stupor and after lunch I dozed with drooping jaw in the hotel lounge. I once wondered what rubbish roams through the mind of old people, marooned between meals. Now I know!

Pain from the past flooded my mind as helplessly I relived a passion of long ago. It had started with the usual high hopes and ended with the usual rows and recriminations. Frantically I added up the pluses and minuses to my ego – the hits I'd scored and the hurts I'd endured.

'Must it end like that?' I cried out in my sleep (perhaps someone saw my lips move).

'Not necessarily,' said a familiar Voice within me.

'But I can't change what's gone,' I said.

'You can always alter the ending,' said the Voice. 'You're alive so the story hasn't stopped. Try and see it again through my eyes.'

I forced myself to try, because if I didn't do a repair job on the past it would poison my present and my retirement. All the sums I totted up began to seem so silly. Even if you lose someone you've loved, a bit of them has become part of you, and when you think you hurt them, you're the one who screams. This means that you've got to forgive if you want to be forgiven, because they are only two sides of the same coin. I no longer knew any name or address where I could find forgiveness, but I'd make it up and do a good turn to someone else instead.

'Charity always cheers up a sad story,' said my uninvited Voice.

'I won't behave like that next time,' I promised.

'Aren't you too far gone for a next time?' said the Voice with amusement.

'With God all things are possible,' I answered sweetly.

'Hmm . . .' said the Voice and abruptly changed the subject. 'Look Lionel, there's a time for penance and a time for pastries.'

Sure enough, a hubbub filled the lounge and I woke up. There was tea on the house for all and we got three biscuits each.

My friend Fred

My friend Fred stared up in awe at the skyline of the small Spanish town. It was punctuated by towers, turrets, crosses and crowns like the quills of a porcupine. Church façades reared up around us crowded with sad

47

stony saints, which looked as if they had been carved out of Common Market butter, their girdles and gridirons frozen in a high baroque breeze.

I like my religion penny-plain, but Fred likes his tuppence coloured. 'There'll be nice nooks and niches in them,' said Fred, 'with saints and such.'

'I prefer lights,' I said, 'to focus my faith. Eternal lights, candle lights, I don't mind, provided they're not electric.'

'Would you care to pray with me, Lionel?' said Fred.

'I don't mind if I do,' I replied. 'Though services don't switch me on, I'm partial to prayer.'

But our assault on the supernatural was foiled because all the church doors were bolted. 'It's a liturgical lock-out,' said Fred gloomily and went off to find a cooperative cleric.

'We've got to find Sid,' he said when he returned.

'You mean El Cid,' I said knowledgeably.

'I don't know his initial, Lionel,' said Fred humbly, 'but you knock at the side door and ask for Sid the sacristan!'

But Sid, L or otherwise, must have been locked in the sanctuary because he could not be found. Passing clergymen said the lock-out was the fault of the socialists, the capitalists, General Franco, long lunch hours and high insurance premiums. Nothing could be done about it. Nunca, nunca! – never, never!

At the tourist office they tut-tutted and suggested another sort of spirit – less holy, more helpful. The sherry shops were always open whatever the time. Siempre, siempre! – ever, ever! No trouble!

They were right, there was lots of room at the inn. The way to the wineries was wide and the waiters welcoming. First they showed us how to make the stuff, then they sat us down to drink it – chin chin, bottoms up, on the house.

'I'm shorry about your shaints,' I said to Fred.

'Don't give it another thought, old chap,' said Fred. Then looking up at the lights shining from the bottles in the bar he said, 'Lionel, can't you focus your faith on those?'

I glanced up at the glinting bottles, promptly invoked God's presence, and experienced some minutes of deep peace and piety.

'You'll never lack lights now,' said Fred contentedly, 'because when the places of worship shut, the pubs start to open.'

I returned from the holiday to my office. I was debilitated by dieting away those hotel meals and irritated by the pile-up of post. A visitor came to see me unexpectedly and I hardened my heart and, whatever the reason, that's a sin. Now if there had been an eternal light on my filing cabinets or even a glinting bottle to focus my faith, it might have made all the difference. But there wasn't, and I realised it's not enough to look at a light in a synagogue or even in a bar, you have to carry your light inside you.

A habitación is not a home

In Spain a hotel room is called a habitación – which is exactly what it is, a habitation, but not a home. But over the years I've had to live a lot in hotels and tried to work out how to make my habitación homey.

Until the fifties, hotels and guest houses were not concerned with cosiness. The former did not consider your comfort but your status, and the latter sometimes locked you out during the afternoons whatever the weather. Many didn't try to be cosy or homey. Their ceilings were high and the wardrobes were cavernous, just right for a party game of murder. I can't say I ever slept well in them, because the wardrobe doors used to creak open and give me nightmares.

They were also cold. If there was a coal fire you could choose where the limited heat was required most – was it frozen frontals and baked backside or vice versa? If your room had been 'modernised' a thin red filament replaced the coal, giving a little less light than the light bulb and a little more heat.

There was a long, long trail winding to the loo and the bathroom, and in the morning you journeyed hopefully along the landing. It was like a treasure hunt. You followed a thin line of carpet with stained surrounds, through passageways, upstairs, downstairs, and through swinging doors, till you arrived at a line of souls outside a door, tut-tutting and timing the fortunate, relieved occupant on the other side.

They were a shaggy lot in flannel pyjamas and hairy dressing-gowns. The gentlemen glared into their shaving mugs and the ladies looked pained, for their hair was twisted into cruel clips. They were real ladies for they solved the social problem by simply pretending they themselves did not exist, and as the gentlemen were gentlemen this curious convention was respected.

Only foreigners ever tried to converse at such a time in such a place – and this was considered coarse, having regard to the tacit purpose of all concerned.

Hotel life taught you morals as well as manners. After this lesson in delicacy came a lesson in courage. When you got in (and in the nick of time too) you had to heat the water. This often meant striking a match, throwing it into the geyser, and then rushing for cover behind the wooden towel horse while the machine exploded into life. You learned patience and fortitude as you sat, goose-pimpled and pink, in a luke-warm water puddle wondering when it would be decent to call it a day and dry yourself out.

This excursion down memory lane may not be relevant to modern hotels, which are almost embarrassing in the lists of comforts they provide. Machines are everywhere and even if they are too technical to use (like the slot machine for sex movies) at least the intention is good, and you can use them as executive toys. You can have whatever gives you pleasure: mild porn on the screen, or a nice pot of tea. The trouble is that a man does not live on peanuts alone, and sex is, at best, a part-time activity, and with most people a little goes a long way.

When I get to my hotel room I sit back for a while and try to settle myself in with a whisky and a bar of chocolate. I remember that a habitación is a place, but home is a state of mind. So when I have finished the crumbs and thrown the silver paper away, I get out my prayer book and recite the long Grace After Meals. It does the trick, and I fall asleep contentedly on my strange bed.

Dutch courage

In Dutch cities religion has to take its place among all the other passions of people. Apart from a few show pieces, the churches are set among the ordinary houses in the street, between cafés, bookshops and shops selling anything from sex to souvenirs. And yet I learned something there which I never found in London – and it wasn't sex or souvenirs, it was just simplicity of speech, or honesty. I didn't even find it in a seminary or a synagogue or a church, but in the devastating directness of Dutch daily life. You can find truth in holy places but commonplace honesty is a rarer bird.

I went to Holland just after the war. My school had

advertised a holiday there, where we children could view lots of cows and clogs in clean air, and be respectful over the Rembrandts.

The holiday never took place because of an understandable lack of enthusiasm among the children. We had all had enough clean air in the country during our evacuation, and what we wanted was city dirt and dust and dance halls where we could wear our new ties from America. They had girls painted on them and, if you were lucky, would light up with the help of a battery in your breast pocket.

The school regretfully notified my parents that the holiday was off, but I intercepted the note, said polite farewells, and that is how I arrived in Rotterdam, marvelling at my freedom, but not sure what to do with it.

I was rescued by a Dutch family who gave me my first lesson in false politeness, or fibs. There was a plate of cream cakes on their table, a treat I hadn't had for years.

'Have one, Lionel,' they said. 'Oh, I really couldn't,' I said primly, perfidiously licking my lips. (My parents had told me never to accept at once. You took one after two refusals.) And then to my indignation the plate was passed on to the other end of the table. They didn't seem to know their lines. They should have responded, 'But Lionel, you must have one.' I would then say, 'But really this is too much!' They would then add, 'But, please,' and I would answer, 'Well, a small one then,' and take the biggest off the plate.

The look of that cream cake has never left me. I can still recall its creamy, fruity juiciness, for in memory it is mine. I still think of it whenever I am tempted to part from the truth. If I put on the style in a pulpit, for example, and pretend to believe more than I do, or say more saintly sayings than I have a right to, then that piece of pastry is an awful warning against pretence, whether for the sake of piety or politeness.

Another shock came at a dinner party. The gentleman sitting next to me said quite simply, 'I don't like you very much.' Emboldened by the bracing Dutch air, I answered equally simply, 'I don't like you either.' After that we chatted amiably, and when we meet after all these years we still greet each other reasonably, though without rapture.

In England, the dreadful thing is that the more people dislike you, the more polite they are, which is very confusing if you aren't quite English. They have a clever combination of unpleasantness and politeness no continental can match.

Anyway, that is why I suddenly bought a cheap excursion-ticket to Holland and set off rejoicing from Liverpool Street Station.

When I got to Amsterdam the cafés were almost collapsing with the energy of their clientèle, who were bellowing the fast waltzes of the place. Everybody was telling everyone else exactly what they thought of them, and I did too. Instead of trying to love mankind, I decided instead to be straight with my neighbour. It's harder than you think!

A Brit abroad

Many years ago I went to America and enjoyed it hugely. I had never met such hospitable people in all my life. For some reason they decided I must have culture, so I was walked through their museums, galleries and opera houses of which they were very proud. I tried not to be a spoil-sport, but after my first acre of Old Master I broke down and told them candidly that once you had seen one, you had seen them all. My feet were killing me and I asked politely if I could have a break from Kulcha.

What would I like to see? they wanted to know, and I told them I wanted to meditate in a supermarket for a whole day. Kindly and unquestioningly, they took me to a medium sized, suburban one, and left me to it.

I spent a happy day. There was a shelf with thirty brands of maple syrup, and I gazed and gazed and licked my lips. There were all sorts of wonders unknown in post-austerity Britain: tubes of liquid smoke, pop-up popovers, squeaking cereals, and lovely pictures of breasty mommas – Italian, Negro and Jewish, all smiling succulently on cake mixes, passion pie, devil's food and peachy-weachy.

There was an enterprising quality about American food which charmed me. Pineapple popped up with peanuts in the most extraordinary places, tucked away in the innards of bleeding steak, or lurking in lettuce leaves, or moistened with melba sauce. I cannot vouch for the taste of these goodies because I do not have a good head for alcohol (it makes me sleepy) and the Martinis were stronger than any I had sipped as a student. This was not puritanism on my part. After all, I had a decanter full of British sherry, and 'cup' flowed freely in my bedsit. But gin was an expensive sin and beyond my means.

Eventually, I found my spiritual level in a doughnut parlour, beside a motorway, built in the shape of a doughnut three storeys high. I felt very sophisticated in my doughnut, slouched at night behind a bar, making backchat with the boys and consuming blueberry, pumpkin, sugar daddy, and southern style doughnuts with cream and coffee.

An engine driver I got to know asked me why I didn't stay over there. I bit into another doughnut and puzzled it out, for I found the people, their cuisine and the landscape quite lovely. I told him it was because they lacked one freedom which I couldn't do without. This puzzled the parlour and the boys asked belligerently what freedom they could possibly lack which I, a Britisher, found so essential.

It was very simple, though hard to explain. I wanted the freedom to be a failure, or since that is rather strong, not to have to be a success, because that makes life very tense and worrying and I am anxiety prone enough as it is. In America the pressures were so much stronger and the competition so much tougher that it wasn't easy to stand aside or say 'thank you very much but it's really not my sort of competition', and sit it out. In the old country it was possible to be genteelly poor, and second class was still not sordid. I could be eccentric without being a hippy and I could walk to the cut price grocery in my carpet slippers without my congregation feeling betrayed, or shown up, or let down, or whatever. Competition had a funny effect on religion too. It was as if everybody had changed roles. The believers never stopped talking about fund raising, nor the unbelievers about the state of their souls. Together they packed the pews or queued for the couches at their analysts. At home nobody was very interested in 'getting on', either in this world or the next.

Actually, I did get offered a job in America, medium by transatlantic standards, but beyond avarice by mine. I thought it over but decided I had to come back. I had bought a second hand 'steam' TV set, you see, and couldn't afford to miss *Coronation Street* any longer.

Faith Food

Love

Love bade me welcome: yet my soul drew back,
Guilty of dust and sin.
But quick-eyed Love, observing me grow slack
  From my first entrance in,
Drew nearer to me, sweetly questioning,
  If I lack'd any thing.

A guest, I answered, worthy to be here:
  Love said 'You shall be he.'
I the unkind, ungrateful? Ah my dear,
  I cannot look on thee.
Love took my hand, and smiling did reply,
  Who made the eyes but I?

Truth Lord, but I have marr'd them: let my shame
Go where it does deserve.
And know you not, says Love, who bore the
  blame?
  My dear, then I will serve.
You must sit down, says Love, and taste my
  meat:
  So I did sit and eat.

(George Herbert)

I do not just encounter love when I dine or prepare food. I also bump into my own greed and vanity. William Blake saw eternity in a grain of sand. I see the judgment and the enjoyment it brings over a cuppa in a café or kitchen. Watching fellow diners in a restaurant is a revelation.

Salad days

Many years ago I met a man in hospital and each December we celebrate our survival in a restaurant. One year I treat him and the next he treats me. It's the only time we ever see each other, so we try to do each other proud.

We sipped sherry and looked over the menu. It was his treat and he suggested the salad bar. It was great value. You paid for a big plate and filled it as high as you liked, but you couldn't go back for more. He pointed to a table loaded with poultry, and peanuts with pineapple, and fish, smoked, fried and souffléed, and beetroot and bottled cherries and lumps of pale pâté.

We watched a lady who had selected portions of tuna, tomato, potato and paté. She paused and brooded over little patches of plate which peeped between the piles. After a moment she suddenly plunged back to the bar and frenziedly firmed up the foundations on her plate, soldering the potato salad with sausage and salad cream. She licked her lips, ladling on beetroot, beef strips, celery and assorted citrus. On top she balanced turkey thighs and chicken wings, in which she wedged the cherries.

At the table she plunged in her fork just before the tower tottered. We watched fascinated. The weight of the wings and the thighs cemented the lower layers on her plate. Beetroot oozed like blood, staining the celery,

'Would madam like a doggy sack?'

and mayonnaise clogged the crevasses. For a few forkfuls she persevered, probing the impacted mess like Schliemann excavating for the true Troy. Then she looked pensive, and pushed the impacted mess away. She ought to have started all over again, but this is not allowed in 'luncheries' or life.

'I haven't got the spiritual strength for the salad bar,' I said sadly. 'But you'd know when to stop now,' said my friend, 'being a religious man.'

I remembered how I had shoved and pushed at the sales and said, 'No. Greed makes us all grabby now – rich and revolutionary alike, poisoning pleasures and prayers. We can't enjoy what we have, because we're so worried about what we haven't. In the East governments suppress religion; in the West they don't have to, they pervert it by goods and gifts.'

I told him a story of a pious lady who was strolling by the sea with her daughter. A great wave crashed over them, sucking the daughter into the surf.

'Oh God,' she cried frantically, running up the beach, 'please give me back my daughter!'

Her prayer was answered, for there was another great wave and little Betty, battered and bruised, was restored

60

to her mother's side. But the mother again ran frantically down the beach. 'What about her hat,' she screamed, 'what about her hat?'

The waitress interrupted this touching tale. 'Will you be taking the salad bar now?'

'No, I can't manage it. I'll have fish fingers and french fries.'

'We'll do spiritual exercises,' said my friend consolingly, 'and firm up our faith to try the salad bar next year.'

A meal composed of kindness

Some friends invited me to dinner, and knowing I might be going 'vegi' once again, though I hadn't got there yet, served me some substitute chicken woven from vegetable fibres, and in the warp and woof of the phoney fowl they stuck a plastic wishbone. It was excellent, as was their seafood cocktail, composed of parsnips not prawns.

But I do not wish to mislead you. Some imitations are not that good. They look fine, and taste fine at first, but their aftertaste, difficult to disguise, is the giveaway, which is why wine tasters swill their mouths out.

This is true of holy as well as profane nourishment. The same caution applies to the milk of human kindness as to the sort you consume from bottles, granules or powder. Loving words can cover a lot of looniness. Greed can be disguised as generosity, and just because the letter-head is religious it doesn't mean that God has dictated the contents. Taste, and see for yourself that the Lord is good, the psalmist tells us, don't rely on the promotion.

On a lecture tour, I tasted both the true and phoney forms of friendship.

At an inter-faith meeting, I sat demurely on a dais, flanked by other spiritual artistes, rather like animal turns in a humane but holy circus. The compère introduced us one by one and I listened with satisfaction and surprise as he enlarged on my virtues and attainments. He singled out my sincerity, with which he claimed personal acquaintance. The introduction over, he turned towards us and said in a hoarse whisper, 'Which of you guys is this limey rabbi from England?'

But I also remember arriving at a little airport in the Midwest in winter. I was met as usual by a smiling hostess, who whisked me away happily. European rabbis were scarce in those parts and she'd got one! All the local leaders would meet me at her dinner party tonight, she told me. She had been practising French cooking for weeks, to make me feel at home. It was the summit of her social success and she sighed blissfully. When we got to her house she showed me to my room, glancing at me as she went out. She returned carrying a heavy tray. On it was a bottle of Bourbon, a bottle of ginger ale and a platter stacked with sandwiches, pecans and cookies.

'But if I eat these I won't have room for your delicious dinner,' I said, overwhelmed.

'You aren't coming to my delicious dinner,' she said flatly. 'I guess you've gone through this routine too many times, and you're tired. Have a good rest, and you'll meet folks tomorrow.'

'But what about your party?' I asked.

'They'll just have to make do with my French cooking,' she said. 'You're our guest, you come first.'

Well, the Bourbon was good but I've never forgotten the taste of that milk of human kindness, whose good aftertaste still lingers across the Atlantic. It was the real thing.

The real thing comes costly, of course. Unlike synthetic substitutes, you pay a high price for it. The parable of the Cohen cornucopia makes the point so well.

The Cohen cornucopia was a jewelled brooch which flashed like a lighthouse on the bosom of Mrs Cohen as she moodily munched her smoked salmon at a banquet.

'Gee, it's lovely,' exclaimed her poor neighbour who sat beside her.

'It sure is,' said Mrs Cohen, 'but there's a curse or worse on one who wears it, a price that must be paid. I know it from experience,' she said sadly.

'What could be the curse that accompanies it?' breathed her companion, thrilled.

'Why, the curse is coming closer. Meet Mr Cohen!'

Hash!

I had just finished writing a book of prayers and I wanted a holiday from holiness. So I thought I would lead a life of pleasure instead and give a party.

My mates could provide the ale, I could cook up some hash, and then we would play solo, a game which is as humble as hash and just as satisfying. I only needed spuds and onions from the supermarket, because hash is like God's love, you can mix into it all your mistakes.

In the supermarket, raspberry juice was on special offer, the bargain of the week in the yuppie world. It seemed too good to miss. Why didn't I surprise my friends with my nouvelle cuisine – an airy-fairy mousse, wrapped in superior spinach leaves, all soused in raspberry juice. I thought I would show them what I could do, even though they preferred quantity to quality, with lots of red cabbage and pickled onions. I realised I would also like to show them not just what I could do, but what they couldn't do. I knew this notion wasn't nice, but that didn't make it disagreeable.

I hesitated and bought some Sauterne to supplement the ale. I wavered again and ended up in my kitchen with half the ingredients for one sort of menu, and half the ingredients for another. So I opened one of those severe cookery books which look like textbooks for medical students, and with a ruler followed a recipe grimly, line by line. But somewhere along the line my ruler slipped and skipped a line which said, 'Turn the oven down to 200°F.'

By the time I discovered what I'd done, there was no dish for the diners to dine off at all, just a few spoonfuls of gourmet gravy. Perhaps they wouldn't show up, I thought hopefully, and in my mind unjustly branded them in advance as ingrates.

The doorbell rang. I hoped for a moment they would go away but it rang again and I went to greet them with a smile on my lips and hatred in my heart. As you can guess, the evening was not a success. They gulped their gravy and waited for more, but there wasn't any. They said they wouldn't stop for solo, not in the mood.

I had made an unholy hash of it because I had been grabbed by greed when I was shopping, and seduced by snobbery in the scullery. I had forgotten that God sits in judgment in supermarkets as well as in synagogues and you can profane His name in your pantry as well as in your vestry. You can't take a holiday from religion, and God remains real, even after you've stopped writing about Him.

Like lots of religious people I get trapped by formalities. I think I know it all because I've read a bit of theology and say my prayers. But the crunch doesn't come when you expect it, penned off in your pulpit, but when you don't. Then you don't have to believe that sin poisons pleasure. It's obvious!

But I suppose, dear reader, you are eating breakfast as you are glancing at this. I can hear you say, 'That rabbi is a bit heavy reading at breakfast, Fred. I don't think all this religion goes with rashers.'

'Oh, I see why dear, he doesn't have rashers, so he wouldn't know.'

Well, I do know, because there are lots of Jewish stories which spell out the priority of food.

A Jewish gangster in prohibition days was paying his old mother a visit. He rang the bell and was mown down in an ambush by the machine guns of a rival gang. He fell down, riddled with bullets, as the door opened.

'Momma,' he whispered, 'they got me.'

'Shh son,' she said. 'Food first, we can speak later.'

Poor fish

Well, the party's over, and clothed in a plastic pinny over a decrepit bathing robe I survey the scene. There are white-wine stains and red-wine stains, so it reminds me of the Wars of the Roses. And it also reminds me of the Blitz.

I used to push my way after the air raids through similar rubble for pieces of shrapnel. I found a lovely piece once and put it on the mantelpiece to show dad. When he got home, black and burnt from fire-fighting, he looked upwards and then threw me out of the kitchen window. My mother landed on top of me. My shrapnel was a live incendiary bomb! We made it into a cigarette lighter, but lost it again when we were blown up by a bomb of a different type.

Once a scavenger, always a scavenger, and I examine the debris to see if I can make up a mixed hors d'œuvre. Well, there is a slice of salmon, lightly dusted with cigar ash, a truffle with a toothmark and a pickled herring still wearing its head, but not much else.

I had expected something better, so I retire to an armchair and count my blessings in the year just gone, the real ones not the obvious ones. That year I was able to spend an evening in my own company, without rushing to a telephone and chattering to everyone I could get hold of. I was beginning to feel free at last from my own compulsions. I also learned to make an omelette which was firm outside and runny inside. I wondered if I could transfer the same delicacy of touch from my pans to my passions.

I also started to take my time in prayer. I didn't rush in with tormented tirades. I looked around and listened to the rumble of traffic, to rustling robes and bird song, and the sounds of this world carried me quite comfortably into the next. I found there was a therapy in small tasks and if I woke at night I meditated over the washing up.

But against this, a friend of mine was very ill. We meant a lot to each other but had never got it together. Between us we knew a lot about eternal life, but not so much about this one. We had been innocent or naïve, whichever word you prefer to describe for the pre-pill, pre-porn generation. I don't think it was just our fault. As soon as you know how to cope with one part of your life you are moved on, and just when you really know how to live, you've had it.

So there's a lot of anger inside me, but I can't put it into prayer because I'm not really religious enough, just politely pious. If I could insert some expletives in my own private liturgy in the New Year, both God and I might heave a sigh of relief.

Life is full of hidden catches and traps, and this is what jokes are about and why they matter. At the funeral of some wealthy worthy, a guy was sobbing his heart out. The rabbi went up to him and tenderly put his arm around him.

'You're crying because you were so close to him,' he said.

'No,' said the mourner, 'I'm crying because I wasn't.'

Well, that's life! I asked a Christian minister I know to explain the doctrine of the Fall, because I was curious.

'It means,' he said, 'accepting you're an imperfect person in an imperfect world and acting accordingly.'

And that is what I did, for it suited my situation. I blew the ash off the salmon and added my toothmark to the truffle. But I covered the herring head with a serviette because it didn't look so sanguine, poor fish!

A communion cup of tea

If you drop in on another religion, you always feel a bit uneasy. There are so many words you can't understand and so many hidden traps. When do you sit down or stand up? When people process to the altar or ark do you join in companionably or sit glued to your seat in the back row, looking stand-offish? Whatever you do seems wrong or rude. Are you intruding on something private or are you really welcome? It's quite a problem, and I've seen lots of people hesitate outside a synagogue or church or temple, wondering whether to go in, but without enough courage to do so.

Of course, the texts outside tell you about loving each

other and all being sisters and brothers together, but we've all learned to take official words with a pinch of salt. It's so easy to talk about loving mankind, but it's more difficult to welcome one stranger.

I wandered into a strange church a few weeks ago because I wanted to say a prayer for a friend of mine who had died. It seemed her sort of place, a church where she might have worshipped. I said a prayer for her, but I felt an outsider as everyone lined up for communion, and I sat on, an unbaptised and unbelieving Jew.

As soon as I decently could, I tried to hurry away but in the church hall I was waylaid by a woman who put a cup of tea in one of my hands and a big slice of cake in the other. 'Come on, lovie,' she said, 'eat it up, we're not as bad as all that. I made the cake myself and I'm not one to count the currants.'

It dawned on me that another sort of service was taking place in the church hall, not as formal as the first but with all the same features. This time ladies ministered to me with buns and biscuits. And because they gave their food with a good heart, it was a kind of communion, though cosy with lots more calories. The old minister from the church came up to me too, shook my hand, and refreshed my cup. This time he didn't preach about kindness, he just did me a kindness – it was the best sermon of all. I suddenly saw all the people in the hall as God meant me to see them and I will never forget them as long as I live.

'Have a slice of my meat pie,' said the first lady. 'I made it myself.'

'I can't,' I said, 'I'm Jewish.'

'Well, that's a real shame,' she said. 'It's one of my best.'

I suddenly confided what Grandpa Goldstein used to say: 'Lionel, if you're a pious Jew in this world, God might let you enjoy yourself like a gentile in the next.'

She smiled and I became garrulous and confident enough to tell her a joke I remembered from the war, for both of us were of that generation.

In 1942, when everything was 'off', a man went into a butcher's shop and asked for a pound of fillet steak. To the astonishment of the assistant, the butcher answered politely, 'I'm sorry, sir, but we've run out of steak today.'

'Well, what about chump chops?' said the man.

'I'm afraid there's no chump till next Tuesday.'

'Well, I'll make do with liver,' said the customer.

'I'm really sorry,' replied the butcher politely, 'it's my mistake, I just forgot to order it.'

When the man had left, the assistant turned to the butcher. 'Why did you put up with such nonsense?' he asked angrily. 'Doesn't he know there's a war on? What stupidity!'

'But oh, what a memory,' said the butcher wistfully.

We all sighed thankfully as we saw the abundance we now enjoyed. God had bonded us, glued us together with gooseberry jam and other sticky delights. When they learned I was a rabbi they asked me to say a blessing, so I said, 'God bless all who give food with a good heart – the tea trolley ladies, those who push meals on wheels, and those who give cakes and cuppas to bewildered strangers. May God serve them His food in paradise.'

Rejoice

In the West misery comes easier than merriment to religious people – you can hear it in the dying fall of clerical voices. There's more whining than wining and no one I know dances before altars or arks like David.

This makes it difficult to get fun from religious festivals. Indeed, lots of people give a sigh of relief when they are over.

The problem is most acute at Christmas and the Jewish Chanukah, which occur in the same month. The problems they present are visible even under the mountains of soap, scent and talc that cover them. Their message comes through with difficulty. Here are some practical ways of bringing out their piety, as well as letting loose a cascade of cards and presies.

Foaming Begonia

At Christmas time I wander into charity shops looking
for presents. There's a sour smell from the rags, bottles
and bones, but the debris of other people's lives is
haunting and compulsive and I am spurred on by greed,
for I might discover a second-hand Rembrandt among
the ruins, almost as good as new. There are certainly
some thumbed paperbacks inside which I would not be
brazen enough to buy in a bookshop.

But standards of taste are rising. There on the shelves
was a nice book, just like the one I had given to a dear
friend. I reached up for it, and found it was the one I
had given to the dear friend – now less dear than before.
He had been in such a rush to recycle it even before the
revelry began that he hadn't even erased my greetings.

If you engage in such practices, then you should at
least have the courtesy to suppress the evidence. I had
to make the same point many years ago to a client in my
office. In his sleep he embraced his wife fondly and
called her cuddly names which were heartfelt but not
hers. Even moral considerations apart, I said, he should
desist from philandering. He wasn't made for it, not
being the strong silent type, asleep or awake. 'No,' I
added severely, 'another milky drink at bedtime was
not the answer to his problems – matrimonial or moral.'

But it is difficult to know what to do with the manna
of scraps, sachets and bath salts which descend on us

at Chanukah and Christmas time. I look over my loot and wonder what Judas Maccabaeus would have made of a bottle of Foaming Burmese Begonia bath essence. Not much, I should think, he was far too macho, nor would there have been sachets of it in any Bethlehem boarding house, let alone the manger. And what about another bottle containing concentrated bergameot, cucumber and other legumes? Do I use it on my body or my hair, or just pour it over a mixed salad?

If presents can only be objects, it becomes very difficult to know what to give the Almighty at Christmas. What do you give to a Being who has everything? You can't recycle your scraps, sachets, and salts on Him. Even if Him is a Her, as modern theologians tell us, it makes no difference. Cleanliness may be next to Godliness but it is not the same – oh, no no no!

And if you try to fool God, you only fool yourself. So it's no use throwing the coins in the collection plate up into the air and saying piously, 'Lord, you keep what you want, and I'll keep the change that you leave behind on the ground.' Yes, I know that is an old joke and you've read it or heard it before. Well, so has He. It's so old He probably invented it.

74

It's also no use offering up one of those manipulative prayers: 'Lord, if you help me win the Premium Bonds, I'll give a lot of the lolly to charity – if it be Thy will of course and pleasing in Thy sight.' Be careful, be careful, sometimes your prayer is answered in such a back-handed way, you'll wish you had never made it.

I think the only present you can give God is your attention, though I realise that after basting and baking the bird, boozing and bursting into song, you don't have much of that left. But a moment of it in the kitchen, freely snatched from the turkey and transferred to God, may be all He wants and be very precious in His sight, better than all that Foaming Begonia of which He has quite enough already thank you, since He created the lot.

Self preservation at Christmas (A rabbi's advice)

Mary was an old lady who lit our Sabbath fires when I was a child. She had been a real lady once, but had fallen through a black hole in the social system because of bereavement and booze and now earned a few shillings switching on lights for Jewish families, which was forbidden to them but permitted to her.

She was a Shobbos Goy, a lowly Sabbath gentile, but she knew more about the practical side of Jewish piety than anyone else. She taught me that religion is about food, fire, and holidays, as well as doctrines and holiness.

I have become a sort of Shobbos Goy in reverse, for I've cooked for Christian contemplatives while they got on with it, and washed a busy bishop's smalls. And these are my practical tips for Christmas, which some look forward to but many dread because they are single and solitary.

You have to decide beforehand if you want to be alone. If you don't, I suggest a Christmas house party at a retreat centre. They're cheap, cheerful, and might just squeeze you in. They're not hotels, of course, but homes from home, which means you will have to help wash up. But you get good gossip in pantries, because people aren't too pious there. In any case it's nicer singing carols in a chilly chapel, than sitting in a boozy bar with a jukebox, belting out *Y Viva España* – though you can find God there too and a lot of kindness.

If you can't get in, ask your minister to sort out some other singles and celebrate together. After all, you're only going to eat with them, not marry them. If you're a pensioner, proposition another pensioner in the post office queue.

Don't get worried about the food. You may still have time to brew a gallon of bedsit Bordeaux. And if you cheer up your pilchards with pineapple-bits and your beans with chilli, the result looks happy and Hawaiian.

If you feel forlorn at a party, ask to help out in the kitchen. That's where the best people congregate and where you get the best cake and counselling.

If you do decide to be alone, remember there are lots like you and you aren't a failure. Sit back in an armchair with some port and pâté, and work out the difference between being alone and being lonely, because they're not the same. And if people aren't crowding around, God might be able to get to you.

It's not enough watching new born baby-dolls in a

department store manger. Some new charity has to be born in you too. Otherwise Christmas, or any holiday, just means gift paper, talc and executive toys – most of which will end up as junk in the charity shop. So why not pick up the phone and just say Happy Christmas and patch up an old quarrel. It's as good a proof as any that God's got in.

Mary was the first real Christian I knew. She practised her faith but couldn't explain it. When she tried to explain its doctrines as well as its practices she confused me completely. For years I wondered why the prophet Elijah popped down my chimney and why rabbis rode on reindeer.

A rucksack of memories

I've forgotten now whether we got gas masks before we left or after we arrived, but we were all issued with a kit list to give our parents. It was September 1939 and the great evacuation was on. I had a rucksack, but the moment my mother filled it, her mother, my grand-mother, unpacked it and refilled it. When she had done this my grandmother's crony did the same. All three then reproached each other in a variety of languages. They started off in English, but quickly progressed to Yiddish which was fruitier. 'May all your teeth fall out except one so that you still feel toothache,' was one of the more memorable curses in that language. But even Yiddish was inadequate because my survival and salvation were at stake, so they had a ding-dong in such rare and rich Russian it even silenced the spectators.

My assimilated mother had conscientiously filled my

rucksack as the authorities required (socks, smalls and labels). My grandma had turned this out and replaced it with a kosher roast chicken, a bottle of sacramental wine, another bottle of pickled cucumbers, a box for milk foods, a box for meat foods, an amulet against the evil eye, and a thick slice of smoked salmon.

Her crony, who vied with her in piety, granted that she meant well but what could you expect of white Russian Jews? (She was Polish herself.) 'Peasants,' she whispered in my mother's ear. Out flew the dead chicken and the salmon, and in poured prayer books, a Pentateuch and assorted objects of piety. The only thing that survived was my amulet, which she considered a prudent choice as I was going to live among gentiles.

When I tried to put on my rucksack it was so heavy I fell over. But no one would give way on the contents and I only got to school with it supported by two old ladies gabbling in a goulash of dialects on each side and by my mother in the rear. When the whistle blew and our school marched off both grannies let go. I fell over, flat on my back, and a rugger scrum developed behind me and on top of me. So, scarlet with shame and embarrassment, I was evacuated into a gentile world.

In this clumsy way I lurched from the snug, warm, Slav-Jewish world I knew, and fell quite literally into England, real England, not the watered-down version I had peeped at from the frontiers of Aldgate. It is difficult now to realise how grey it was in the first years of the last war. Even if there is a recession, our towns and villages are dotted with lights, and oranges and bananas are things to eat, not things to remember and describe. There is colour around, not khaki. In 1939, first the wrappings disappeared on the chocolate bars, and then the silver paper, and finally the chocolate itself shrank and almost vanished. Eggs did vanish and so did onions, and one winter we subsisted on turnips and carrots in all the ingenious combinations urged on us by Lord Woolton. (Some still remember the recipe for Woolton Pie.)

Food was on everybody's lips because it wasn't in their bellies. Housewives swapped tips for scrambled dried egg. Some made it into a sludge and steamed it over water, some 'fried' it with a wisp of marge. If you coloured potatoes with beetroot you could make a Sunday roast (sort of).

Everybody who remembers that time had his or her own special grumble. Mine was socks. They were grey, lumpy, coarse things, and we were taught to darn them at school. I couldn't master it, so sewed up the heel and toe holes instead. The resulting blisters were so painful I was forced to walk on points.

But as my colleague Rabbi Gryn learned in a concentration camp, you can live without much food but you can't live without hope, and hope was in very short supply at that time. The convoys were being sunk in the Atlantic and my father was issued with a pike to resist the Nazi tanks, for invasion was expected daily and sometimes hourly.

One grey morning in this grey time, in a foggy, unlit market town, I wandered into a church because I had nothing better to do. (Like most evacuees, I was pretty aimless and lost.) It was Christmas time and the congregation had conjured up out of the austerity, colour, candles and a crib. I was dazzled and trotted round the church because the glitter reminded me of Selfridges where I had once been taken as a treat.

I examined the statues and the crib, and got into conversation with an elderly lady who tried to explain to me the difference between the Christmas story and the fairyland in an Oxford Street store.

What stunned me was something she took for granted. It had never occurred to me before that you could come to God with your eyes – that you could 'see' Him. Like most Jews, I was used to the idea of hearing God, of listening to His voice and attending to His word – but 'seeing' – well, that was mind-blowing! Even Moses at Mount Sinai (Ex 33: 23) had only seen His back and here was I, according to the lady, looking at His image face to face! It seemed incredible and I asked her if she was kidding me.

Another problem I had was saints. The word 'saint' wasn't used so much among Jews. Adjectives such as 'saint' or 'holy' were strictly reserved for God, or very occasionally for the Jewish people, hardly ever for individuals. We had of course our own share of the good and the great and the martyred, but they were never pictured or used as they were in the Church, and I couldn't get accustomed to the idea.

I also never worked out how much of it was 'real'. Was the star 'real'? Do animals kneel down? Did angels exist, and did they have wings like the pictures? But I did understand that beneath the glitter on the surface there was light and love for their devotees, and in those sad days after the fall of France this took a lot of believing. I didn't believe in such things myself, but I believed in the lady's belief, and that worked almost as well.

The lady in the church was struck by these questions. What sort of Christian was I, she asked. I told her I wasn't any sort at all. I was a Jew. 'Oh,' she said thoughtfully, and she put away a little book about Jesus she may have intended to give me. She thought a bit. Then she told me to wait as she wanted to get me something. She returned with a white sugar-mouse which glittered and had a pink tail. She gave it to me and said she would pray for the Jews in Germany who had nothing else but prayer to help them. She had nightmares about them, she said.

I went back to my foster home, clutching my Christmas mouse. I also had nightmares at that time, but shepherds and sugar-mice and stars began to figure in them occasionally, driving away a bit of the despair. So something began to glow in my greyness – I had made contact with kindness, though it wore different dress and spoke in strange symbols. There was goodness outside my ghetto as well as inside, and this, like dried egg, was a great discovery.

Winwood Street

Unexpectedly I had a free day, and decided to take a journey in time as well as in space. So I bought a ticket to Whitechapel and for a while wandered among the stalls, fortified by some tea and a bagel of boiled dough. I even began to back-chat in the Yiddish, cockney sing-song I had spoken as a child. I marvelled it still remained, buried under the layers of the suburban, yuppie, Oxford, BBC and pulpit dialects I had spoken since.

I turned down a side street behind the grim grandeur of the London Hospital (I noticed they had tried to tart it up but that forbidding façade resisted all frivolity). Threading my way instinctively like a hunter through the alleys and backstreets, I came unexpectedly to a great block of flats. Either it was wrong or I was wrong, said my memory. I asked three passers-by but they had never heard of the street I was seeking. But a woman in a sweet shop had. Her mother told her there was once a little street where the flats now stood, but she couldn't remember its name – had probably never known it. I did.

The name was Winwood Street, Stepney, London, E1. The last war had blown half of it to bits and scattered its inhabitants. Then the planners had come and obliterated the ruins that were left. But for the first ten or eleven years of my life it had been home. I had learned about love and life from the women gossiping in the tiny shops, and from my grandmother (God rest her soul!) I had learned about God. The street had been my school and my entertainment. Its pavement was my seat in the stalls, and its roadway my theatre. It exists now on a map in my memory. These stories are its makeshift sketchy memorial, for they were born there.

Lessons on the pickle barrel

When I was a child there was a shop at each corner of our block. There was a greengrocer, a grocer, a baker, and a sweet and tobacco shop. They didn't just provide goods, they were also social clubs, gossip centres, informal citizens' advice bureaux and 'schools' which supplied the local children with an unofficial education about people and politics which our official teachers never gave us.

I used to help out at the grocer's shop which was run by a wizened old lady. She paid me with scraps of smoked salmon (the brownish bits next to the skin), broken chocolate cup cakes, pickled cucumbers, and legends.

She used to sit me on the pickle barrel, throw me some scraps and say: 'Darlink, now listen! Why do you think, darlink, you have a crease between your eyebrows, above your nose?'

I was caught on the hop, for my official teachers never explained the 'why' of things, just their 'how'. 'But you've got one too,' I said, finding the same crease in her old wrinkled face.

'Yes, darlink, I've got one too, and who could have put it there, because we were born with it?' She shook her head portentously. 'It must have been an angel.'

'But why, but why?' I shouted from my barrel, for this was more curious than any multiplication table.

'Before you were born,' she said solemnly, 'this angel told you everything that would happen to you in life, about all the people you would meet, all the important things that would happen, and all the lessons you would learn.'

'So why don't I know it all?' I said disappointedly. 'Why do I bother to go to school?'

'Ah,' she said, 'now I come to the little crease. After the angel has told you such things, he takes a hammer made of real silver and taps you between the eyebrows, so you forget everything the angel has told you. That is why you have such a crease,' and she shook her head, threw me another sliver of salmon and shooed me out of her shop.

But it wasn't all. Many years later, when I was up at Oxford, I puzzled over my feelings. Some were explained by sociologists and some were just textbook examples from any primer of popular psychology. But some feelings didn't seem to have an explanation. Why, for example, did I sometimes have a feeling that I had done whatever I was doing before, that once long ago I had been in the same place or situation. I shrugged it off but the sensation was strong. Also, when something important happened to me or when I learned something that wasn't just college cleverness but really significant, I felt as if I had known it all along. I hadn't learned it, I had just remembered it. It was as if long ago I had been told everything important that would ever happen to me but someone had tapped me on the head and I'd forgotten it.

Instinctively I felt for the crease between my eyebrows. It is sad that the little corner shops are going. There are no longer pickle barrels to sit on, or counters to lean on. And who can take time off from check-ins and calculators any longer and teach little children legends. So traditions die.

A slit of light

After I was born, my mother went to hospital and I was brought up by her mother. The latter was only in her fifties but already very old – a peasant woman to the end of her days. Like her cronies, she was swathed in black shawls, waddling along on rheumaticky legs with slits cut into her shoes to ease her bunions.

In accordance with tradition she wore a sparse wig to hide her female charms, lest her grey wisps inflamed the passions of pious men. Under her wig she hid her savings, two brown ten-shilling notes, fought for penny by penny.

She earned them from casual labour in hotel kitchens where she piped cream over cakes. Sometimes she would risk her job and peep through the swinging service doors at the dancing diners, wondering what life was like if you didn't have to worry about the rent. She stayed there till a chef shooed her away.

The two ten-shilling notes were my inheritance, she never tired of telling me. Her aim in life was to get me out of the ghetto, through those doors, to join the beautiful people beyond.

Well, I've made it as she wished. I write books. One day I might winter in Benidorm and buy a bungalow and I'm grateful granny gave me the shove.

But with the comfort and leisure you buy things granny could not foresee or ever comprehend. Boredom, for example! You need spare time for that and granny never had any. Also the pointlessness of life, once you get what you want. That wasn't granny's problem either. On the wrong side of the service door, there were no

'She always had a head for money'

senseless suicides, only occasional attempts at murder. Nor was happiness her problem, just survival and respectability. But happiness is a peculiar thing. If you run after it, it runs after you and you never meet. But if you forget it, it just happens. Whether she had it, I don't know, but she never worried about it like me.

Such worry would have bewildered her, but she would have grasped this story of two grannies whose husbands made it and who met on the heights of Highgate.

One said, 'How's things?'

'Fine.'

'And business?'

'Fine.'

'That big car, your car?'

'Yes.'

'Nice car! And that kid, your kid?'

'Yes.'

'Nice kid!'

The other then asked her questions.

'And how are you?'

'Fine!'

'And business?'

'Fine.'

'That coupé there, your coupé?'

'Yes, my coupé.'

'Nice coupé. And the kid in the back, your kid?'

'Yes, my kid.'

'Nice kid.'

'He can walk now, but thank God, he don't have to!'

All this ran through my mind as I sat in my dinner-jacket at the top table in a distinguished hotel, about to give an after-dinner speech. I toyed with my glass, then raised a forkful of mille-feuille to my mouth, keeping one eye on the chairman. But my other eye was fixed on a shaft of light in the swinging service-door. I could just make out another eye, as black as granny's, staring into the splendour.

I raised my glass to it. It blinked. The swing door swiftly closed, and the slit of light dwindled into darkness.

Divine dating

He used to pay a call upon my mother's parents in Stepney every Sabbath afternoon. He wore a frock coat and a high hat and in his hand he carried a large red umbrella. This he held like a bishop's crook, for its presence was not a sign of impending rain but of forthcoming marriages. It was his sign of office, the insignia of his profession. He was the local marriage broker. His reception matched his status. He was ushered into the parlour, not the kitchen, and only the best tea set was good enough for him.

My mother's parents had discussed his visit the whole week, and they sat stiffly on either side of him, grandma trying to look a lady (which she was) and grandpa trying to look pious (which he wasn't).

All the young people in the family were introduced to him, like débutantes being presented at court, and even I, though still a child, was not missed out. I was a long term investment and had to be hauled out from under the bed.

Gravely, their prospects were discussed. There was a possible match with the girl round the corner. Her piety made up for her pimples.

He shook his head sadly over the dowries my grandparents could provide, saved up in a slump from household pennies. He didn't think he could get our girl a real tailor, or a cutter. A factory hand perhaps – an older man, of course, but kind!

This was how they were married off. There was no compulsion but romantic love was frowned upon as indecent. Only an arranged marriage was respectable and likely to last.

When the young couple were introduced I was grabbed from the street, washed, scrubbed and unwillingly appointed chaperone. The young people (often in their thirties) paraded slowly down Whitechapel High Street, and I brought up the rear. I was six years old but already a guardian of decency. No wonder I became a minister, after this training. If my unmarried aunt went out for tea, she stood in the doorway of the teashop and solemnly counted the number of men and the number of women. If the former outnumbered the latter, I was sent for to protect her honour. I was bribed with pastries.

It was such a pure world – an adjective scarcely understood now. Over every brass matrimonial bedstead hung the occupants' marriage contract, framed in gilt, to show whoever dared to doubt (I never met one) that what went on was under the direct supervision of heaven.

A couple came to see me in my office. They had met through a bureau and were embarrassed about it. Did I disapprove? They were apprehensive and they sat primly and waited on my answer.

They brought back my youth, for that was how my elders met. In that pre-war world, love was not something that happened, it was something that you earned by your loyalty through the years. It could not be the beginning of a relationship – that was to confuse it with something trivial like being 'in love' – it was the end, the prize, the summit. I told them I would and could help them and they smiled uncertainly. I would chaperone them to a teashop, I said, if there was still a pastry in it for me!

Wonders!

When I was ill as a child my mother took me to the doctor, but her mother rushed instead to her miracle man to get me an amulet against the evil eye. One of them must have worked, because I'm still here.

After 1939 I never again met a rabbi who could work miracles. They vanished in the war. Some were gaunt mystics, leading godly lives in tumbling tenements; some just religious rascals, like the one who trotted after Grandpa Goldstein when he went to the bookie, to bless his bets. Some had been ordained by holy hermits, some had just ordained themselves. They were treated with caution by the respectable rabbis of the establishment.

Their miracles were bizarre but always had a hidden laughter in them. There was the saint who claimed he could walk between the rain drops, and another who could turn the Sabbath into a weekday so he could smoke whenever he wanted. I had my suspicions, even as a child, because they couldn't perform the miracle of a decent meal for themselves and granny had to provide it for them.

But their words were wise, and when I close my eyes I hear their sad lilting Yiddish of long ago.

'A father can feed fifteen children, Mr Goldstein, but will fifteen children feed one father?' It's a pity parents don't recognise such truth sooner.

'What gives God pleasure, Mrs Goldstein? When He sees some poor starving beggar pick up a pound in the gutter and hand it in to the police. That's what gives God pleasure, Mrs Goldstein. That's what He's like.'

Yes, that is what He is like, but it has taken me a lifetime to recognise it.

At my mother's wedding they sang out, 'Hetty Goldstein, Hetty Goldstein, now a knife-edge is too broad a bed for you both. When people are old the whole world is not wide enough.'

Grandpa, grandma and their family lived in a tiny tenement and my Uncle Abie, who was built like a six-foot gorilla, slept with his legs dangling out of the window. Grandma complained to her miracle man who told her an old story:

'A poor good woman, just like you, Mrs Goldstein, went to her rabbi – such a wise man – weeping, "We live in one room, my husband, me and my children, and we fall over each other."

'"Buy some chickens!" said the sage. The astonished woman bought some. Later she returned ever more miserable.

'"Rabbi," she said, "the chickens cluck and the children scream and my husband complains I'm going mad!"

'"Get a nanny-goat!" said the sage. The woman sobbed but bought a goat in the market.

'The next day she was back. "Rabbi," she said, "your advice is too hard for me, I'm not holy enough."

'"I'm sorry," said the rabbi. "Sell the goat and get rid of the chickens."

'After the Sabbath service, the woman rushed to him. "Without the nanny-goat and chickens, life's so wonderful," she said, "so much space and quiet. I've never had it so good, thank God."'

If only I had pondered such sayings sooner, how much easier my life would have been. All I can do is recommend them to you. If I had taken them to heart when I was young I would have saved myself so much trouble!

Pleasures of the poor

A clergyman I know whispered sadly into my ear at a meeting. 'There's nothing worse than poverty, you know, Rabbi Blue,' and he shook his head fiercely.

I thought about it, and then I shook my head too because I did know it and it just wasn't true. It's the kind of thing middle-class people say if they've been brought up in a garden suburb and then got sent to a seminary after Oxbridge. If you lived in poverty you knew there were many things much worse.

You could survive without your money, but if you lost your respectability you couldn't live with your neighbours, and if you lost hope you couldn't live with yourself.

Although I am now middle class, and have fought my way up to suburban heights, in my childhood I lived in a street of failures. We must have been failures because if we weren't we would certainly have lived somewhere else. My brave father sold ice-cream from a barrow in a recession winter, if he was lucky, and my aunt worked in sweat-shops and lost a lung.

But in that street you could survive poverty if you hadn't lost your pity, and even make it festive with a little piety. My mother's mother, who was a mine of misinformation, told me that onions would purify my blood, carrots would make me see in the dark, fish would make me clever, and garlic was good against vampires. But she also taught me some other things too: how to be poor with decency, how to prevent my envy from eating me, and how not to be taken over by my own anger – and God knows she had enough to be angry about.

We lived in Stepney, where the plumbing was pretty grotty and the health inspectors tut-tutted over the bugs on damp walls, though there was little they could do about it. But our spiritual hygiene was fine, as high class as you'll get in any garden suburb.

Poverty taught you a lot about failures and about festivals. Every year, during the Jewish festival of Chanukah, we used to crowd into the scullery while Grannie Goldstein made potato pancakes in honour of the Maccabees. Why potato pancakes? I don't know. It was tradition. The Maccabees could never have seen a potato but we saw little else, because they were cheap and cheerful if you cooked them with imagination.

She grated raw potatoes and a piece of onion, drained off the water, and mixed in a beaten egg, cracker crumbs, and salt and pepper. She then fried tablespoons of the batter in hot oil, and as they came out of the pan we fell on them.

While she fried she sang pious songs, and we shouted back not so pious refrains. 'Mo'oz Tsur Yeshuosi,' sang

gran in Hebrew – 'Strength and Rock of my Salvation.'
Led by my Uncle Abie, I bellowed out, 'The rabbi's in
the cupboard and he can't catch me.'

I remember bits of another Yiddish song about Stepney, much beloved of gran, who keened away about
'Stepney, Whitechapel, where the holy word is sent,'
and led by mother, my aunts shrieked out, 'Where our
Sadie is a lady, and her Stanley is a gent.'

As we got high on potato pancakes the songs got less
disciplined. Gran was fond of a hymn about the miracles
of some holy man she was partial to. Our nice non-
Jewish neighbour had an unauthorised version of his
miracles, which we adopted with glee: 'He goes to the
cinema, where gentile men and women are.'

If dad sold his ices (and he made us a living in
the darkest days), we ate the pancakes with pickled
cucumbers, or apricot jam, or apple-sauce. If he didn't,
we had that delicate dish of the down but not outs –
potato pancakes, served with mashed potatoes. And if
you think that's a funny thing to eat – well, laugh and
try it.

Success
and Failure

My successes have never got me very far. Though I was not very clever about Life, I was considered a bright child and this easy brightness persisted through my university and seminary years. I got full marks for an essay on Adam Smith and I had a knack with Aramaic verbs, the more irregular the better. Why Aramaic? Well, most of the Talmud and some of the Bible is written in it, and Jesus spoke it and so did all his family and apostles. But no one has ever asked me about either Adam Smith or Aramaic verbs, and if I tried to talk about them I would soon be talking to myself.

To my surprise (and initial annoyance) what people wanted from me were my weaknesses. They liked to hear about my clumsiness and how I fell into a grave and off a pulpit and the terrible faux pas I used to make at international conferences. (They were speaking about this world and kingdom come, but because of my bad German I thought they were talking about East and West Germany, and made a speech based on this misapprehension. It caused considerable comment, which gratified me, but this changed to fury after the pfennig dropped. I left hurriedly and was not invited again.)

Late in life the penny has dropped for me too, and I

have ceased to be an intellectual snob, though there is always the danger of becoming a spiritual one.

We can never know our successes and failures. Only God can distinguish which is which. Some He works through and they bring blessing. Some remain as arid and unfulfilled as certificates won at school for subjects we scarcely remember.

Here are some of my 'successes' which came about through clumsiness, anxiety and cupidity. The final effect is funnier than I fancied at the time.

A piece of potato

Not long ago, I got a piece of potato lodged in my eye (no, I do not know how it got there!). The eye was bandaged and blinkered, and I walked round London, bumping into street furniture and saying 'pardon'.

My appearance became even more piteous when I slipped on a piece of fried fish, although I only wanted chips, and got a knock on the knee. This resulted in my being issued with a stick. Together with my bandaged eye it made me a spectacle and a conversation piece, as fellow Londoners took it for granted I must be hard of hearing as well – although their logic still escapes me.

On the whole, people were very nice to me. I was given precedence in Harrods' sale and a lady stood up for me in a train. I was fed with buns by a troop of foreign Boy Scouts who did it as their daily deed. The buns were fresh, and I felt like a bear, though much happier than the bored ones in the zoo.

An American lady from a Park Lane hotel helped me across a road I did not want to cross, but she was interesting and amiable and I liked being led, though it took me a long time to get back to the place where I'd started and I had to wait till she stopped looking back to check on me.

I seemed to raise enormous feelings of guilt wherever I appeared. Nobody knew how to cope with me on the crowded bus. As I stood in the gangway, a contented young couple got into a heated argument – their first perhaps – and it was over me.

'The poor doddery old thing,' said the girl. 'Why don't you get up, dear, and let him rest?'

I resented her adjectives but to get a seat I was prepared to swallow my pride, so I quivered very slightly to support her words.

Her companion was made of sterner stuff, and gluing himself beside her whispered urgently in her ear. I could not hear his words but I could reconstruct them from her reply. 'Oh,' she said doubtfully, 'it's healthier for him if he's upright – it's better for his bottom.' She blushed prettily as she delicately repeated his words.

I quivered again, anxious to see who would win this cosmic struggle between good and evil.

'And also,' added the young man, sensing his advantage, 'if I got up you would have to sit next to him, wouldn't you, and you don't know where he's been.'

'Well then, perhaps you're right about his . . . posture,' she said, weakening. 'I wonder if he's clean.'

'Can't be,' her swain said reassuringly, 'grubby as a goat,' and he gave her another hug.

With a sensuous sigh his girl gave up and said, 'You're probably right, dear, you always are . . .' The bus stopped abruptly in the West End and I was decanted, indignant at all I'd endured.

It was quite funny really. After all, I was not seriously hurt. They prised the vegetable away from my eyeball and for a while I ate Chinese take-away, not fish and chips. I got attached to my stick and had to be shamed into giving it up. I hooked groceries on it and it did good service in queues. I also used it on door knockers, but then I thought what it was like really to be disabled in London and have to get about. People are nice but they're not consistent – they just can't keep up their generosity when they're pressed, and if you are disabled, that's hard.

Financial blues

It was morning. I opened my eyes and turned on my transistor. There were hurricanes and bad harvests in a remote part of the world which should have concerned me but didn't, because I don't have enough love or imagination. The announcer continued with the financial news. There had been a fall on the stock market – not a crash but a hiccup, and straightaway I wanted to dive back into sleep. There go my savings and my security, I thought. Why had I been so greedy and forsaken those dull saving certificates?

Although the fall was only a financial hiccup it made a lot of people like me a bit sick with self-pity. But it's nonsense to think there are such things as secure gambles in this world or the next.

My financial advice is not worth studying, but I can

dispense some of the spiritual sort, because you don't have to lose your soul with your savings.

Firstly, about spiritual hygiene – don't let your losses embitter you. Losses and gains are just figures on account sheets – less real than your own feelings about them. Don't dwell on them – give them to God.

Sometimes I wonder what we can give God. After all, He's got the lot. Only our losses and hurt feelings can equal the sacrifices which are mentioned in the Bible.

Then, people were into goats and grain (like Common Market farmers) and when their goats went up in smoke, so did their capital. Knowing how to make sacrifices is as important for your sanity as your sanctity. Happiness comes when you know how to give, and giving up is only a special form of giving. Sooner or later you will have to give up everything – not just what you have but what you are, and by giving up your losses now, you get some good practice for harder times ahead.

Secondly, a word about investments. Be careful where you invest your heart, for if your investment breaks your heart will break too. That's why businessmen jumped off their balconies in 1929. Without their investments they thought they didn't exist. Don't invest your all in promotion or even in a person. Invest it in good deeds, says the Talmud. You will enjoy the interest in this world and your capital awaits you in the world to come – which isn't a bad bet.

Lastly, don't get trapped by things which are none of your business. Two Jewish businessmen were on a safari holiday journeying through a swamp. A leathery reptile wound itself round one of them. 'My God, what's that?' he screamed. 'Don't ask me,' said the other, 'you're the one who's into handbags!'

Radio religion

A pulpit is a special sort of place. I process to it wearing special clothes while sopranos sing. My feet are on the level of my listeners' foreheads, so I speak of high matters in a voice so grave I sometimes give myself a fright.

Sermons from above are uplifting but are they relevant to life below? I preach one thing, I know my congregation keeps another, and they know I know that they keep another, and I also know what they don't know but suspect, that I'm in the same boat.

Radio religion isn't like that. I get up at five thirty in the morning and haven't much time to clean up or contemplate – it's a prayer or a shower, not both. In the studio they look like me, because they've been up sorting out the news since the early hours. But then some loony bungs a bomb into a bar and they have to start over again. Perhaps it's the magic BBC coffee that keeps them so calm and courteous.

I don't process into the studio, I slink into it – not to talk of the dogmas we don't share but about the common experiences we do. I have to tell my own truth straightforwardly and there's no time to tart it up. The greatest sin in radio religion isn't graven images or coveting your neighbour's ox, but delaying the eight o'clock news.

Walking to the tube afterwards, occasionally I buy a bun for breakfast and munch it in a hospital chapel nearby. Religion is real there too, so that's where I think up thoughts for my own day. Outside in the corridor, an old-timer, festooned with drains and drips, whispers from a trolley, 'Hey, rabbi, have you heard this one?'

'Surprise me,' I say, interested.

'Well,' he says, 'there's this daughter who's visiting her old mum in the medical. "Ow are yer?" she says, and the mum says, "Daughter, that new chaplain over there cheered me up something wonderful. 'E's a real man of God – 'e is." "But Mum, yer need new glasses, that ain't the chaplain, that's the doctor." "I'm pleased you said that, daughter," said the mother all virtuous. "I thought at the time 'e acted rather cheeky for a chaplain."'

I choked on my bun, and putting his arm through the drip he patted me kindly on the back.

When I first went into religion I prayed for a special revelation, a vision of a new heaven and a new earth. But now I know I only need to notice what's in front of my nose in the old one. God gives me all the uplift I need through professionals working in tension without temper, through sick people making wisecracks as their own bodies crack up, and through the people on the other side of the mike who take time to listen to God talk, when God knows they've got enough on their hands.

Little things

I want to thank God for trivial things, the ones that get me up in the morning. I look through the papers but the news is so heavy. They are throwing bricks and bottles in Northern Ireland and no politician has a nice word to say for another in public, which is a pity as privately they are probably old pals. Anyway, I can't take it. Why don't they give us some cheerful news instead? I would willingly pay a penny more for news which helps to get me up. Hasn't someone been dealt a complete suit in bridge? That's what I'd like to read! Or that someone has sussed out a way to prop up a soufflé and keep it up, or they've stopped whopping each other in Wapping because somone has heard a whip-poor-will. Such things are equally real and just as significant.

Some people steady themselves with breakfast in bed, but then you need someone to make it for you and who would do that? In any case, you would only get lacerated by toast crumbs, or lose a piece of poached egg in your duvet, or upset your coffee in your navel ('my cup runneth over'). What about a glass of Grande Cuvée, when you dive back under your duvet? (That's poetry, mind, and I made it up myself.) The only consolation is that a piece of poached egg is less slippery than a slice of smoked salmon, but then, if you could afford smoked salmon you wouldn't feel so sad and soggy, would you?

I decide to make my own entertainment instead, and be a suburban Orpheus. A nice nun gave me a recorder a while ago. I can only play 'I love little pussy', but I am proud of it because it's the only tune I've almost mastered. So I tootle my tune as I lie in bed, and though the dogs howl in the street I am so pleased with myself I get the courage to poke a foot out of the covers.

It's no use starting the day on the tough stuff, such as opening up an income-tax form, or worrying yourself about 'the source of suffering'. Such things are just not on when you're fragile. Do something sensible, like transferring the contents of one drawer into another, or arranging some plastic flowers, or looking for the least smelly socks in the laundry bag. You need a bit of success to soldier on.

And for God's sake, don't be too dismal in your prayers! Why do you have to list all your mistakes? You've had some successes too. After all, you've survived – you're still here, if only just. Why depress God as well? He has enough to contend with, without you being damp and droopy too.

Yes, a lot of things can go wrong. There may be damp in the drawing room, but it's only outside you not inside. And you can't be the only one. There are people who can cope with it, if you lift the telephone. There's no need for you to be damp as well as your walls.

Give yourself a little lift. A glass of good wine in the morning isn't a cure for whining, as toothpaste ruins real Tokay. So why not try tinned custard? It's a childhood delight, but as it's a.m. not p.m. you don't have to pretend to be a gourmet or a gourmand, even if you knew the difference.

And even if you know you're not a saint and never will be, well, that's no reason to give up. Say a little prayer. Unlike salami, you don't measure it by length. Do some little kindnesses as well if you are not up to the supreme sacrifice – they will probably be more appreciated. If someone asks the time, make sure it's the right time, and no temper mind!

Journeys in Faith

Although believers have always tried to love each other, they have never really liked each other. So occasionally they burned each other, for the best of motives.

I was blown into other religions because of the Blitz and, though bewildered, found I enjoyed them. Perhaps it was because of the war, but there was more welcome than I expected. Lots of people like to boast that their own religion remains unaffected by such contact. Mine wasn't, and I'm glad of it. I was able to learn from a universe that was bigger and richer beyond all belief than my own parish piety.

A clumsy lot!

A Jewish paper considered my humour was helpful on the whole, but wondered if I had inherited my jokes from my grandparents along with my memories. Well, this is true of many of them. Someone else said he could tell them better. This is also true because I am not a funny man, only someone to whom funny things happen, because I was born clumsy.

But clumsy people like me possess a truth hidden from the capable and clever. We know that not much good is done by us – we aren't efficient enough – but God makes it up and does His will through us instead, making something out of our silliness. That's why we don't take ourselves so heavy, dear.

This is what happened one freezing winter morning in the choir of a monastery on the continent. I had gone there because God had gone out of my life. But that medieval deep freeze didn't bring Him any closer, and I wondered what a Yiddisher boy like me was doing in a place like this, surrounded by moaning monks. I ought to be listening to the *Today* programme instead, eating a Yiddisher breakfast of herrings and lemon tea and onion pretzels. So while the monks sang their psalms, I salivated over slices of salmon.

In desperation I looked across the choir and saw the pale face of a novice, rapturous, with eyes closed in the shadow of his cowl, obviously experiencing those holy happenings that ought to be coming my way and weren't. But I had an idea that was cute though caddish. While paleface meditated on God, I decided to meditate on him meditating, to get some uplift. Whenever I thought of food, I took a piggyback on his prayers. And it worked.

I met paleface many years later at a conference. He had gone up in the world and was now Father Paleface or Monsignor Paleface and he gave me a bottle because he could never thank me enough, he said. In the chapel, as a novice, all he dreamed of was bed, and bed made him think of something else and something else had made him think he was in the wrong place. But one morning he had looked up and felt my gaze burning into him. An unbeliever had obviously sussed out his sin and judged him, and he was ashamed.

After he confessed to me, I said, 'Snap' and confessed to him. I opened his bottle and poured out a strong tot for him and one for me. It was quite ridiculous. We had converted each other by mistake when neither of us had anything to give.

Clumsy people like me know God in a special way. He is not only their King and Judge and other macho things but also the joker in their pack who laughs with them when other people laugh at them, who heals their bruised pride with His good humour.

Abie was a clumsy man and whatever business he was in went bust. So he prayed to God in the synagogue, 'Lord, this is Abie, I've done it again and lost everything. Please help me win a thousand pounds on the Premium Bonds, it's my only hope. I'll be back next week to collect!'

No answer came from heaven that week or the next.

But three weeks later, in the synagogue, Abie pleaded again, 'Lord, this is Abie, I hope you remember me.

What about my win of a thousand pounds on the Premium Bonds. I hope you haven't forgotten.'

And suddenly a heavenly light played upon him and a Voice spoke gently from above. 'Abie, my son, I haven't forgotten, but do me a favour. Can't you help me halfway, and buy one Premium Bond?'

Lunatic and loving

The train rushed through Rugby and swept on to Stafford. I saw some cooling towers on the horizon and asked the man in the next seat if I could lean over and look through the window. He seemed surprised because it wasn't tourist country, just midlands' mess, but I wanted to see the retreat house at Spode before they closed it in a year's time and it was turned into a supermarket, or a hamburger heaven, or a lunatic asylum.

The building was rather lunatic, built in Victorian times and ornamented tastefully with turrets, towers, and minarets, no expense spared. It was lovely, like St Pancras Station. It had long echoing corridors, just right for a game of murder, and more stonework than a suburban cemetery.

The building rested on a coal mine, though rested is not the right word because it never stood still. The canal which I looked down into on my first visit, I looked up at on my last. Holes could open at your feet, which provided sermon subjects of the sadder sort. One day the lake leaked out through a crack and a merciful, muddy monk dashed about rescuing grubby, gasping fish.

'It wouldn't be so bad if we weren't in a smokeless zone'

At Spode they tried to trust people, which is not lunatic but unexpected. Sometimes they got stung, but not often, and I learned there that people rise to the occasion and became what you believe they are. They gave the rabbis the key to the bar and told them to tot up the totals themselves. They let you meander on about mysticism in the kitchen at midnight, and didn't measure out the marge or count the cups of tea. Their trust worked wonders. At the bar a lively group social-ised amiably with members of a cricket club, and rabbis found refuge in a jam session, playing the kazoo.

You weren't chivvied in the chapel if you were on a retreat, or made to run a lap round the liturgy. Instead they just let the Lord find you – and at Spode, for me, He did just that.

They also treated religious people as adults, which is rare. I heard a priest sermonise to some novices on prayer, and I waited for the pious patter. I heard this instead: 'Prayer is an adventure. You hope it might help your vocation. I hope so too. But it might lead you out of your vocation into the unknown. You must take the risk.' This was the hard stuff and I didn't miss another word.

Their trust made caution redundant. You could tell jokes at Spode that you didn't dare tell anywhere else, about Scotsmen, Irishmen and Jews, or priests, pastors and rabbis like me.

There was a police raid on a gambling den and three clergymen were arrested. The judge turned first to the priest. 'As you are a man of the cloth, I shall take your word. Did you gamble?'

'Lord, forgive me,' said the priest under his breath. 'No, your honour, I didn't.'

The judge then addressed the pastor and asked him the same question. 'Pardon me, Lord,' whispered the pastor. 'No, your honour, I didn't.'

'Well,' said the judge, turning to the rabbi. 'What about you? As a man of the cloth, did you gamble?'

'Me, gamble, my Lord!' said the rabbi astonished. 'Who should I be gambling with?'

The train sped on and the turrets of Spode were lost in the distance. I decided to tell the joke to the man next to me. It seemed a trusting thing to do. He smiled politely and said kindly that he was sure some people would think it was funny. Well, I tried!

One puzzled pilgrim

I hear that the Pope is going to the synagogue in Rome on a considered visit to improve Christian-Jewish relations.

I also try to do my bit and turn up unexpectedly at the shrine of Walsingham, just before Easter – which is a mistake. I have got the date wrong. Easter usually comes after Passover. This year it doesn't.

Easter is not the most tactful time for a rabbi to arrive at a centre of Christian devotion but everybody falls over themselves to make me feel at home. A kindly priest introduces me to the shrine's taxi driver – like me, by origin a Yiddisher boy from the East End. I am just about to ask him, 'What on earth are you doing here?' when I realise he could well ask me the same question, so I desist.

I am confused. So are some lovely Lancashire mums who clutch me to their hearts, and make much of me. One of them calls me Reverend Father (neither of which I have ever been to my knowledge), but refer mistakenly to a robed and bearded priest as Rabbi. He is a pleasant sort who isn't peeved. They urge me to visit a lady hermit who is very old and very holy and inhabiting a shed in the grounds of the shrine. I demur. I have no appointment and it seems discourteous to interrupt her solitude unannounced. I need more time to adjust because when I'm flustered I only say silly things like, 'What's it like living in a potting shed?' But they assure me she is very patient and perceptive – perhaps I will have more courage next time.

The mums go on a walk and impulsively I decide to join them. Too late, I find out that it is a penitential march on which they recite prayers and hymns, and I bring up the rear. I sing out Amen when it seems suitable but neither my hearing nor my theology are sharp enough and I am exhausted. But a mum with white hair in a wheelchair suddenly tells me I am cuddly, which is uplifting. I think she is too and am moved to offer her some of my milk chocolate (with nuts). We gaze at each other with mutual satisfaction.

Over boiled eggs at breakfast, the ladies talk about God, Life, and Lancashire Hotpot. They are knowledgeable on all three, and I am impressed. I am suddenly surprised by my benevolence at breakfast – it is a time when I can dislike everyone, irrespective of race, religion or creed. I decide that though it is not a miracle, it is certainly a wonder of the domestic sort.

They implore me for a Jewish joke in return. 'There are three mums at an anniversary party,' I say, 'and one boasted, "My daughter has given me a complete kosher kitchen to celebrate my anniversary." "That's nothing," said the second, "I only wanted a picture for the fireplace and my son, as a surprise, bought me a real Rubens." "Ah," said the third, "now my boy goes three or four times a week to the most expensive psychiatrist in town and guess what – all he ever talks about is me, his mummy!"'

I wonder if such humour really works in Wigan. *'Qui sait?'* as the Yiddish saying goes.

Before I go to bed, I sit down in the silence and say my prayers. Around me are a grandmum, a mum, a crippled child, a dad, God, me and another mum. I feel very fond and very close to them all, and I think they feel it too.

I say thank you to God for helping me cross a frontier in faith. It was muddling but worth it. I hope His Holiness feels the same in the synagogue in Rome.

Blown with the Blitz

The old East End of London consisted of tribal lands. The tribes were classified by colour, custom, and cuisine. There was the Irish-Catholic tribe streaming out of shrines and shamrock dance-rooms, genial and generous, but liable to erupt. They were a brawny lot, and the pale stooping Jewish children watched them fascinated but at a cautious distance. It had been said, though no one knew the source of the rumour, that they drank. What, we did not know.

The black coated, bearded Jewish men hung around the garment sweat-shops, or gesticulated outside the miracle-rabbi's door (the combination of piety and pop is not a post-war discovery). Their suffering wives bargained for scraps in the markets and, with their loot safely in the larder, concocted dishes of the highest calorific content known to man. Occasionally they chatted with the marriage broker about their daughter's prospects. Doctors and clerks were too great a prize, but with God's assistance a machinist with a good heart might yet be found.

Alongside these were the worlds of white cockneys who ate eels and black West Indians who ate peanuts and chillies. Little client worlds, too small for full autonomy, clustered around the Greek grocer, the Russian hermit, and the Hindu astrologer.

On the whole, these worlds lived peacefully alongside each other, eyeing each other curiously, rarely mixing.

Take Christmas, for example. I knew the other tribes celebrated it, and even the Hindu astrologer acknowledged it with phonetic greetings in his window. But I was kept a long way from it. My family recognised a certain flabbiness in my character and decided I was no match for the magic and seduction of this festival. Since Jewish families are an indulgent lot, I got presents on December 25th, but was told they came from Judas Maccabaeus, who came down a chimney. A likely tale, I thought, even at that tender age, and I classified December 25th presents with other exotic and unexplained phenomena such as babies, jellied eels, my anatomy, and Karl Marx.

When the war came – the real one of 1941 not the phoney one of 1939 – the bombs rained down on the East End, and blew each of those worlds into fragments, and then fused the fragments together in a strange way. Old tribal loyalties melted and a new tribe was formed, a nocturnal tribe which inhabited the brewery cellars in Whitechapel Road – whose members huddled against each other for warmth as the fires raged round their homes.

It was in the shelters that I first took part in a Christmas celebration. In those vast caverns the children wandered free, joining now one group and then, fickle minded, changing to another. As the crunch of bombs was heard above us, we crossed the frontiers forbidden to us by tradition in all the years of peace. An Irish family sheltered me during one of the panics, and with me as the link, my own family got to know them.

Language was a problem. My grandpa spoke Yiddish and my parents reverted to that language under stress. As stress was plentiful, unlike eggs, onions, marge and anything else you could think of, their accents got broader and broader until even I had to ponder before working out the sense of their remarks. My new Irish friends never bothered much about the sense of things; they preferred the feeling of things. Little gifts of food and booze replaced conversation and discourse quite adequately. My mother rightly said the war had changed everything, and I was allowed to join them in Christmas celebrations in the brewery vaults in 1941. It was then that I first experienced Silent Night, and Christmas pud, and the magic of a crib, and a tiny tot of black liquid drowned in a lake of water.

They got some surprises too. For like the wise men I came bearing gifts – a pot of sweet-and-sour cabbage, some cold potato pancakes, and a charm against the evil eye donated by a pious relation. (I was supposed to wear it to protect me against assimilation and heresy, but I gave it to my Irish girl-friend aged seven, and I hope it has been more efficacious with her than it has been with me.)

One morning in March 1941, we returned to our home after the all clear and found it wasn't there. Like many others we packed the remnants into a barrow and took them to a Government store for the bombed out. There was no point in staying in the East End any longer, an invasion was imminent. So we moved and I never met my shelter friends again.

Something was born among us that Christmas, though it wasn't what our clergy had considered or prepared us for.

Another Yiddisher momma

It was two o'clock in the morning when the telephone rang. The old lady struggled out of bed and hobbled anxiously to the telephone receiver.

'It's me, Momma,' said a panic-stricken voice at the other end of the line. 'Could you come over? I need you!'

'What is it, my baby?' said the old woman, summoning up her strength.

'It's the kid, he's ill again. The au pair is still at the disco and I must get to this all-night party. Oh Momma, I know it's late, but could you come over – if it's not too much trouble?'

'Too much trouble! How could it be too much trouble for my own daughter? Look, don't come and fetch me. I'll get the night bus at the corner – they've never mugged me yet – and I only have to change twice. I'll see to everything as soon as I'm over. I'll look after the house, and some strong soup will help cure the kid's dyslexia.'

'Oh Momma, thank you so much. Little Sammy and I can never thank you enough.'

'Sammy, Sammy? Who's Sammy?'

'Oh Momma, don't be silly. Sammy is your favourite grandchild, and I'm your only daughter, Sadie, who's married to Hymie.'

'I don't know any Hymie. My grandson's an Abie, and my daughter's a Becky.'

'Oh dear!' said the voice at the other end. 'Who have I rung? Are you Hampgate 4321?'

'No, I'm Highstead 1234, and it's after two in the morning. What have you got to say for yourself, young woman, waking up a poor old lady?'

There was a pause at the other end, and once again the voice quavered through the receiver. 'I'm sorry, I'm sorry, but Momma, can you, will you, still come over?'

This joke, like all the jokes about Jewish mothers, is only funny because such mothers existed and their self-sacrifice was real. I remember them from my childhood, swathed in black shawls, waddling with their bunions and blisters to the ritual bath to purify their worn-out bodies, trying to be pious in a strange land, and be decent in their poverty. My grandmother gave her winter coat to a cleaning woman who coughed. My mother gave up her place in an air-raid shelter to a frightened man. Such women gave away their bread in the concentration camps, and kept their homes holy in the Warsaw Ghetto.

So that is why I treasure an old record of Sophie Tucker, on which the last of the red-hot mommas sings of her Yiddisher momma. The song is like treacle and sticky with sentiment, and as she belts it out I get embarrassed. But I can never throw it away, for though the words are trite, they are true. It was the mommas, not the missionaries or the mystics or other religious machos, who bonded me and my generation into my religion.

I think of all this as I sit back in a church. My Christian friends, who have invited me, are kneeling. I look around curiously at the images, which are never found in a synagogue. There is a crib with animals and angels, like toys in a store window. Mary is a Nordic blonde doll with a slimline figure in golden drapes. This puzzles me, for she was another Jewish mother, fleeing a persecution. So she must have been weathered and worn beyond her years, clothed in the faded hand-me-downs of the poor.

I think I begin to understand what my kneeling Christian friends are feeling as they turn towards her in veneration.

Do it Yourself

The older Jewish generations were born into a tradition and they died in it, more or less. (Even their firm faith got frayed by all the twists and turns of a troubled century.) I envied their security and have often thought what a relief it would be to roam no more and be a contemplative cabbage in some saintly patch.

Instead I have had to work out most things myself, putting traditions together like jigsaw puzzles, and trying to be faithful to all the truths that touch me. Boethius knew the score over 1,500 years ago.

Why this division in the nature of things,
This eternal war between truth and truth?

The choice between truth and lies is painful, but not problematic, for few of us fancy ourselves as Mephistopheles. The choice between truth and truth tears our religion apart. Like many in my generation who rejected fundamentalism or guruism, I have had to put together my piety piece by piece. The result may seem poor but it is honest, and tougher than you might credit, for it is tried and tested in my life.

DIY religion

My first congregation consisted of practical young couples. The chairman carried chairs, my wardens washed the windows, and made sure no one turned off the eternal light. They constructed an ark from orange crates and lit it with cocktail lights. They were resourceful but restless. If something was Victorian they remade it Regency, and if it was Regency they remade it ranch house.

Theology interested them less, though they wondered whether it was proper for synagogues to insure against acts of God. The only text that turned them on was: 'unless the Lord build the house they labour in vain who build it.'

I later learned they were do-it-yourselfers, whose hallowed ground was the local hardware store. Inspired by them, I decided to spray-paint my study door. They said it was rabbi-proof, so I never bothered to change my robes.

I stood on a chair, shut my eyes, prayed and sprayed. But no one told me to point the nozzle, and my black robes now had a white bib. In surprise I shot off the chair, sat on the spray and the paint reached parts religion rarely penetrates.

I again ascended the chair, and this time I pointed before I prayed and sprayed. But my two black dogs, scenting excitement, banged on the door and burst in at the same time. Now they too had bibs like me, and we looked like memories of old-time minstrels.

Three changes then took place in my life in quick succession. First I left my lodgings. Soon after, I left my congregation, and soon after that my faith left me.

Finding new lodgings was no problem. I tried to take my door with me, but the new tenant thought both I and my door were unhinged. My congregation easily replaced me with a married man whose wife toted an electric drill. The last loss was more serious. I say my faith left me, but did I have any faith to lose? It was mostly habits I had inherited from others, which disappeared one day quite suddenly as I was taking a synagogue service.

Perhaps I had tried to swallow too many miracles and had thrown up. Perhaps I had tried not to know what I did know and the result was not belief but banality. I was spiritually homeless and kind friends asked me into their faith, but I had no wish to lodge in theirs just because I couldn't live in my own. I was also not up to making up my own religion. A member of my old congregation then said, 'What you need is a conversion job.' So, in do-it-yourself fashion, I joined my own faith to the faith of my fathers.

The religion which resulted was not very beautiful – just a bodge-up, but one I had worked at. Then one day my Talmud fell open on the text, 'Do not call us Thy children, but Thy builders.' I then felt God approved it because I hadn't employed anybody else. I had done it myself.

Time, gentlemen, please!

In the morning paper there was another spate of letters and articles all about God. Some of the writers said He was dead, some said He was alive, but lived only in them. Some said He was dead but She was alive. One correspondent implied He was asleep or snoozing though he didn't put it that way, and another thought he could analyse Him, given the right cosmic couch, of course. He suspected incipient megalomania.

But everybody joined together in a general mope about religion. It was going down, it was going to bits or to the bad in a big way. Ministers were moping, rabbis were recriminating, and bishops were bumbling over its fate. 'Look at the churches,' they said, 'look at the congregations – tiny! Look at the collection plates – pitiful! Not even enough to give the parson one portion of plaice with two of chips, let alone prop up the church tower.' They wagged their heads woefully.

Well, some of it is true, of course. Lots of congregations are declining because, to be honest, they are constipated. It's an odd word to use but quite accurate. You go in, you take part in the ceremonies and say the right words. You sit down, stand up, change hymn books, and sit down again. You kneel, bow, prostrate and otherwise contort. You put your prayer book in, you put your prayer book out, you wave the service sheet in the air, and you shake it all about, but . . . nothing has happened. You aren't any holier or wiser. Was your religious hokey-cokey really necessary? Apparently not – the collection plate says so – why give something for nothing?

But just because some forms of formal religion are dead or dying, this doesn't mean religion has had it. Perhaps everybody is just looking in the wrong place, that's all. You don't have to go to synagogues or cathedrals for religious experiences or ecstasies – in fact you had better not, for they would not be welcome. They might upset the sermon or the choir, and you would be asked to leave.

Quite a few people find divine grace in London supermarkets, which are not planned for purveying such products. A lady on a park bench told me how she was lining up at the checkout, a man was pushing her in the rump with his trolley, and the woman in front was fiddling with her cheque book and credit card and was holding up the entire queue, who were snapping at her, at the harassed girl behind the till and at each other.

Then suddenly, for her, the whole situation turned inside out (that is how she described it), and she felt giggly about the next jab in her rump and experienced a wave of compassion for the poor person on the till. She offered a pen which worked to the lady with the cheque book, and waggled her behind invitingly to present a good target for the trolley of the mighty macho male behind her. It was a giggle, and she was overcome with compassion and love for everybody there. She not only loved them, she liked them, which is much harder.

What did I think of it? she asked. It was a real religious experience, I told her, as genuine as any you find in tracts or in scriptures. But in a supermarket? she said. Well, the spirit bloweth where it listeth – it says so in all the best scriptures and why should we be more choosey than the spirit?

And though people are not swarming into formal services, a lot of people pop in for a little prayer when no one is looking or keeping statistics. At breakfast time, in a little place of worship in a West End side street, there were two or three cleaners, a roadsweeper, some tourists from Park Lane hotels, some secretaries and stockbroker types, a beggar or two snoozing, and me.

I have to repeat that God was alive and well and awake when I met Him last, but He seems to keep odd hours.

Show business

In the pub two men leaned against the bar. The barmaid brought their drinks and one of them stretched out his hand to take up his glass. The other happened to glance at it, and had to turn away to stop himself from being sick. The man's arm was covered with grazes and bites which hadn't healed, and the skin was rough, red and angry.

They started to chat and as soon as he decently could he said, 'Your arm's in a bad way, mate, how did you come by that?'

'Oh, it's all in a day's work. I've got a job at the circus, been doing it for years now and I've got used to it. I scrub the teeth, tusks and fangs of all the animals – the snakes, the seals and the elephants. I give them gargles and wash out their tonsils, to get rid of all the bits of rotting meat stuck in their teeth and the bits of toffee they scrounge from the kids which get stuck in their throat. It's messy work and what with all their bad breath, it sometimes makes me sick too.'

'Well!' said the other, 'why don't you go to the job centre and get something else instead? Perhaps they could find you something cushier, in a poodle parlour.'

The other banged down his glass and eyed his questioner sternly. 'What,' he said, 'quit show-business? Never!'

Well, I've been in religious business for a long time, and it can be quite a dirty business too.

You feel a bit sick when you realise that every army – Fascist, Nazi, communist and capitalist – has been blessed by some religion or other, and people pleaded with God at the same time to punish England and to save the king. It's easy to hijack holiness with tribalism (or nationalism, as we prefer to call it) and organised religion often reminds me of a football supporters' club. It's up our side and down with theirs.

Sometimes the problem arises out of a very simple mistake, which goes something like this: 'I am Lionel Blue, a reform Jew who lives in North West London, and I go to synagogue there. In my synagogue I have a religious experience and come close to God. If you too want to come close to God and have a religious experience, you too should live in a suburb of North West London like me and go to a reform synagogue.' You see the slip, it's so simple, but that's why religious people have killed each other for centuries.

Like most people, I read with fascinated horror the rising toll of Middle Eastern murders. But what is most horrific is that the terrorists (of all types and ideologies) are probably pious people who worship the same God as those they murder.

Sometimes I've thought of leaving religion and making my living differently. Twice I nearly did, but I came back. Why? Because religion has got the guts to make me face a very unpleasant truth. Partial loving, like loving your own group, or tribe, or church, or party, or sex, is natural but not enough. It's only an extension of loving yourself. Unless you try to see the God you love in the people you don't, the killing will have no end. I know this does not feel natural. It isn't. It's supernatural.

So when you ask me why I'm still in religion, I say, 'What! Quit God-business? Never!'

God's personal friends

When my mother is happy she types; when she is angry she bakes. I knew there was trouble as soon as I opened the door. Instead of the merry clatter and tinkle of her typewriter, I heard the oven bang, and a thump as something hard hit the sink.

I recognised the sound. It was the sound of a rock cake denting the dishes, made according to a wartime recipe which expresses her mood and is eggless, fatless and very austere. The rocky lumps are canary in colour and each one is decorated with one black, burnt raisin.

In the kitchen I waited for my mother to speak. She was opening, shutting and brooding over a book of prayers I had helped to write. 'Lionel,' she said, 'you really ought to earn your living in a more moral manner. It's not proper to write prayers for other people. It isn't decent. Why I would as soon pray someone else's private prayers as wear their old undies.'

Then, seeing me masticating her cake, my mother softened, though her cake did not. 'Of course, dear, I wouldn't want you to be a tailor like my poor brother, though he was a boxer too,' she added hopefully.

My mother just does not approve of organised religion. In the past she called us clerics crows, and when I dressed up for a religious procession she told me I looked like Wyatt Earp. But she has a good heart and showed me how to go upstairs in skirts after I tripped over my robes on an important festival and did a header into the warden's box.

129

Yet when I come home on a Friday evening and peep into her room, there she is bending over the Sabbath candles, muttering blessings of her own devising. She doesn't do it for herself. She just reminds God not to forget her own mother who died tens of years ago because she doesn't rate any male reliable, even if He is in heaven.

She is a do-it-yourselfer, who is now too old to hang her own wallpaper. But pays someone to make up her prayers for her! As she says, it isn't decent, and there are lots like her, just as free range in faith.

Some pray after they have been to hospital and seen their loved ones on the rack. They've got to unload their anger on some being lest it makes them ill too, so courageously they bounce it back to the Almighty where it belongs. They wander into empty churches or chapels, because they think God might be lonely too, and need company.

One friend of mine sits in a park every day and pops in a prayer for my conversion. It doesn't get him anywhere, because my mother is praying the opposite in her armchair.

Some pray to steady themselves in the rat race. Some pray on station benches, because they've been stood up by their lovers, which lovers are prone to do, and God's love is the only love left. Such people don't butter up God or nag Him. They pray what they feel, and aren't afraid of being firm in their faith.

Some clerics say God might as well be dead, since so few people go to public service to say official prayers at Him. They often don't notice the growing number of His personal friends who want to chat Him up on very private matters, with no one else around, as in this instance.

Two men bump into each other at the entrance of a place of worship.

'What are you going in for?' said one.

'I'm praying for five pounds because I'm broke. What about you?'

'I'm praying for 500,000 pounds because I'm broke too. Surely you are not going to waste God's time on five pounds. Look, my good man, here are your five pounds. Be a good chap and go away.'

When he had gone away, the other entered and started to pray with great concentration. 'Now that I've got your undivided attention, Lord . . .' he said.

Ordinary Creatures

In the late fifties, the generation after me began commandeering jeeps and jalopies to seek extraordinary perception induced by drastic disciplines at the feet of gurus in the Himalayas (some rather gruesome and some quite Savile Row). They slept on pavements if they were poor or in caves fit for contemplatives with air conditioning if they were rich.

I hesitated and missed the bus to Katmandu and so I stayed put in suburbia, with occasional budget trips to retreat houses.

I just did the ordinary things ministers do among ordinary people. The religious result was the same at much less cost and effort. So perhaps their journey wasn't really necessary. I learned that spirituality can be approached in many ways. You can find the ordinary in the extraordinary or the extraordinary in the ordinary. It's up to you which way round you want it. The former is more fun, but if you get anywhere and don't just get taken for a ride, you discover you have all come to the same place.

God among the paper-clips

Most of the week I sit in a little office in a small backwater of the Jewish world. I write letters, I answer the telephone, and I fill in forms. Yes, it's a 'religious' office because I deal with some of the legal problems of a religious organisation, but whether you're dealing with God or goods, all offices are much the same. Sitting in my chair, I don't have ecstasies or visions. My work isn't spiritual jam or mystical cake, it is my bread and butter – the same as that of any secretary in the City, or clerk working away in one of those tower blocks.

When my clients like me, they sometimes call me Bloom. When they get annoyed with me, they address their letters to Rabbi Glue or Gloom. You can't please everybody all the time.

Now, I suppose you will say – well, this isn't very spiritual! It sounds like the work of an ordinary lawyer or minor civil servant, though without the pay scale of the former, or the indexed pension of the latter. But over the years I've realised it's no use just spotting God on altars or in arks, or sensing His presence in pious objects or clouds of incense, unless I can also find Him (or Her, I hasten to add) among the files and paper-clips and debris on my desk.

Only gradually have I begun to see what God requires of me when all the telephones ring at once, or the memos get muddled up.

135

I don't think He can expect me to find an answer to every problem. When I first became a minister I thought I had to, and nearly had a breakdown in the attempt. Now I know that a lot of problems can't be solved in this life, you just learn to live with them, and try and make your peace with them. I know this is easier said than done, but it's no use supplying false comfort, even if it gets me off the hook. But even in such cases, it is possible to say 'sorry' with sympathy, and to try and listen when the other phone is ringing away and someone is in the waiting room outside.

When I first became a rabbi I thought I would be needed most for talking, and sermons and such. Being young, I liked the sound of my own voice and thought other people might get to like it too. But the most valuable thing I've had to learn (and I am still only a beginner) is how to listen. This requires a patience I wasn't born with but have had to acquire the hard way.

This disclaimer is not modesty but truth. Recently I met a real listener, who has set up a real listening post in Earl's Court – I think it was a coal bunker before. He is also a clergyman, but a different brand from me (he is Church of England) and listening is his vocation. Having talked to him non-stop, I can vouch for its quality. I don't suppose there are degrees or diplomas to be obtained for sympathetic listening, but it is one of the most social works needed in a big and busy city.

It is also a very religious one, and a vocation ready to hand for anyone who can spare a little time in a busy life and make a sacrifice of their impatience and boredom in the service of God. You can listen anywhere. Churches and synagogues are not necessary. An office does just as well. So does a pub, and a bench in a London park.

Red, rough and real

After a service, some people come to see me. They wanted faith, but how to get it? Some hoped that I had a store of it, stashed away somewhere in a secret cupboard. If they caught me in a generous mood, I might let them have a can or bottle of the stuff – rather like in a celestial speak-easy.

Well, like most 'real' religious people, I'm on short rations myself. I have just enough for my next step ahead, though I've learned to make do (it suffices, barely). I've got rather less than most, in fact, because I was never much good at believing. If I swallowed a bit too much, I got spiritual indigestion and threw it all up. Books didn't help that much in the beginning stages. After all, in any paperback bookshop you can buy a hand-me-down ideology to justify any of your leftover childhood aggressions. They make believing seem too easy to be true. But you can't major in modesty or get a degree in goodness.

I caught religion from people, and that's the only worthwhile way I know. If you know how to read their lives, people are like books. It's not difficult because believers become like the God they believe in, and their lives convince even if their words don't – and a lot of them don't have any words.

The only words I ever heard from my Dutch char-woman, so many years ago, I hardly understood, be-cause she spoke in the cockney of central Amsterdam, a rabbit warren of beer and bawd and bounce. I under-stood some of her songs, of course, for she sang senti-mental tear-jerkers about love and loose women and being left out. But these, though pleasant, didn't help me either, though human and divine love are not that different, sharing the same logic.

She used to sing away as she scrubbed with her rough red hands. They never stopped because they always gave value for money. When I was ill they lifted me and fed me. One day, when I am terminally ill, and all of us will be, I hope I will find hands as honest to hold me.

I learned religion from their roughness for they taught me the content of caring and this is more basic to belief than theology, or buildings or belongings. Was she religious herself? I doubt it, for I once caught her carousing in a local café in which religious people wouldn't care to be seen.

But people can testify to what they cannot talk about and teach a wisdom they have no words for. It is the real thing though unfashioned and unfashionable. If you want faith or belief or real religion or other spiritual see-throughs, go where the good people are. Some of their belief might rub off on you. If you use your commonsense and low cunning, you won't get hooked by the synthetic saints, the mad, the bad, or those whose business is instant bliss (at a price). Goodness has a kind of smell, and it is unmistakable. You can sniff it, and something sacred will waft into you.

It's the only way I know.

A dog who got above herself

I knew there was something wrong as soon as I entered the pub. Pretending not to notice, I took my glass to a corner, and waited to see what would happen.

They were indignant about my dog Re'ach. While I'd been away on a lecture tour, people said she had got above herself, and wanted watching. The lady pianist whispered to me, in between her Brahms and her bitter, that they were beginning to call her Bigboots which didn't bode well for a bitch.

I was puzzled, because though Re'ach wasn't bright, she was not given to fantasy either. She was a matter-of-fact sort of dog, concerned with chocs, bones and her plastic ball. If she were human, she would have been happy with her hockey sticks.

Or would she? I decided to test out the situation myself, and returned to the pub later that evening with Re'ach trotting by my side.

As soon as we got through the door, Re'ach dismissed me with a dirty look, and bounded up to the bar. I caught the glances of the clientèle as she placed her paws on the bar and barked for the barman. When he saw her his face lit up, his jaw dropped, and while she gazed into his blue eyes he gazed into her brown ones. Then Re'ach nibbled his ear to remind him love wasn't everything, and he dutifully brought out her bowl.

My jaw began to drop too as he poured into it a tot of sweet vermouth with a chaser of still lemon. 'I don't give her fizzy,' he explained conspiratorially. 'It goes up her nose and she doesn't like it.'

One drinker said to another, 'It's just not natural.'

'Just trying to better herself, poor dear,' said the besotted barman.

Now I began to understand why she kept moving her dogfood closer to the dining-room table and liked to lay her head on a pillow. She didn't want to be an underdog any longer. She wanted to be 'treated natural', like a human being.

'And why not?' I said to the people in the pub.

Religious people too get above themselves, because they want to better themselves. She wants to be a bit human, and we want to be a bit divine – it's the same sort of thing and none of us ever make it. I must look as ridiculous as Re'ach, I thought, clasping my hands together, speaking to Someone who doesn't seem to be there and demanding special foods like bits of blessed bread. Of course it seems strange because it's not natural when we want to get above ourselves – it's supernatural!

To pacify everybody I told them about a prayer meeting where the cantor hadn't shown up. Who would take his place?

'Take my dog,' said a congregant with pride. 'He's got a lovely delivery.' To the astonishment of some and the indignation of others, the dog came forward and planting his paws on the lectern, barked for silence, and then softly chanted the liturgy.

'Wonderful, wonderful! He should become a rabbi at least,' they said to his owner as they congratulated him.

He shook his head sadly. 'You tell him, he wants to become a doctor.'

Private lesson

Every rabbi should have a rabbi, and though mine is dead now, some of him still lives on in me. The rest of him reposes in eternity, if you can trust his sermons, which I do – or rather did – though to be candid they had beautiful beginnings but no endings, which made everyone late for lunch.

As well as being a rabbi he was also a good guy, who could burst into a temper but never bear a grudge. When I was his student, he let me sit in his office, if I kept quiet, while people popped in for advice. There were quite a few visitors, as his faith embraced both fun and failure, and though he preached to people in the synagogue, he never preached at them anywhere. I was prim and prissy, knowing more about liturgy than life, and after I listened to the advice he dished out, I said to him accusingly, 'Why don't you say the same things in your study as you preach in the pulpit?'

'Lionel,' he said, puffing away at his cigar, 'in your pulpit give general rules, but treat everyone who comes to you as an exception. It's not enough to love mankind, you know, you also have to like people.'

And it is true, people never behave as you expect them to, and you have to learn to like them as you find them.

A friend of mine, another rabbi, was called out late at

night to a dying lady. He's a kind chap and he asked her gently what he could do for her. Perhaps she needed comfort or courage for the time that lay ahead.

'Have you some paper?' she said. He nodded and she continued. 'Make sure my daughter-in-law doesn't get my diamond ring.'

He wrote it down. 'Is there anything else I can do for you?' he asked.

'Yes,' she said, 'lots,' and listed her possessions which were forbidden to her nearest, who were also not her dearest.

'Don't you think,' said my colleague gently, without guile or with very, very little, because he is a really nice chap, 'don't you think you need a lawyer not a rabbi?'

The old lady nodded weakly. 'Yes, yes,' she said, 'you're right. But what lawyer would come out so late at night?' My friend laughed, but when I told this tale at a professional meeting, they were highly annoyed and tut-tutted all over the place.

People are great fun and even the dullest can delight. There was no English king duller than George II, devout and dour though he was. When his beloved wife Queen Caroline died, she asked him with her dying breath to promise he would marry again, because she returned his love so much and wanted him to be happy.

'Never, never,' said the distraught king, 'I shall make do with mistresses instead.' The Queen's reply, if any, is not recorded.

I asked a doctor I know about the last words of his patient.

'Yes,' he said drily, 'her last words were, "That chicken . . . quite delicious, I must have some more."'

It is right to love mankind and to feel indignation for those who are forgotten and far away. But on its own such feeling is not enough, because it is too easy to feel.

To do good, you must learn to like people you meet as well, dotty, devious and delightful, just as they are.

A bother of businessmen

Some of my friends and family made it and sweat in the sun at Monte Carlo, and some survive on council estates. My own side of the family never quite made it, though it wasn't for want of trying.

Grandpa Goldstein invented a Kosher catfood, palatable as I can testify, for he got me to try it out on toast. Even puss pronounced it passable. But our rabbi, alas, did not, which was understandable for grandpa was only pious in patches and his praying, like his paying, was sporadic.

My parents leased a shop, like their friends. The shops of the latter grew into supermarkets and super-duper hypermarkets, but my parents' was killed by cattle blight in an affray more fitting to the Wild West than to the tamer East End. It was a sweet shop at the corner of the cattle market, and pa was friendly with the drivers.

'Sell me two loose Woodbines, 'Arry!' one of them shouted as he passed by.

'Come in and have a cornet on the house!' said pa proudly. The driver accepted and, after a moment's meditation, so did his cattle. Onlookers said it reminded them of the siege of Sidney Street, but ma had not remembered the insurance which was a pity, and this explains in part why I opted for religion not business.

There were valid reasons for my choice of vocation (if you can choose a vocation, that is) and some not quite so valid, and one of the latter was that I just didn't have the courage for competition or commerce. Years later, when I watched the small businessmen in my congregation struggling to survive in a recession with a mortgage and an overdraft, I thanked God for my good sense and His. This didn't stop me reminding my businessmen of their shortcomings. They thought what was good for them must be right for the cosmos too, and they also confused comfort with happiness, but conspicuous consumption always peters out. One car is a necessity, two are useful, three show lack of imagination, and four are silly. You can't eat two dinners, though some try to, and make themselves sick. And though people do behave better in a boom, their behaviour in a slump is the religious test.

They put up patiently with my preaching but occasionally let me have it. Ministers, they said, don't create wealth but are wonderful at giving away what they haven't earned, and it was the businessmen who footed the bill. They wondered if I only wanted them for their money, because they had other gifts too. It was their productivity which propped up the world. Was religion as efficient? I thought of my last sermon which had no ending, the dusty dismal temples and my own patchy piety, and I felt ashamed though I didn't show it.

One of them genially, but with feeling, told me this story.

Cohen was on a cruise after a hard year, but the boat went under, and Cohen was left clinging to a plank, suffering from sunstroke and shock. Search parties were sent out and after forty hours began to close in on him. 'Mr Cohen, Mr Cohen,' they shouted. 'Where are you? Say something!' A weak voice answered them from the sea. 'It's all right, it's all right! Don't worry! I already contributed last week.'

Life Studies

When the rabbis of old took time off from law and liturgy to discuss the nature of this world and the next, they compared both to a school. This world was a sort of Workers' Educational Association extension course or an Open University programme. And heaven was the same sort of thing, but holier of course and with higher studies. God Himself would be the teacher, and – oh joy! – no breaks would be needed for food or fatigue.

It is the most sensible comparison I know, for life is not 'a pursuit of happiness' but a learning, and its pupils, as they grow up, find lessons in love and pity all around them.

The following chapters report my own progress in these 'Life Studies'. Some of the lessons were embarrassing and occasionally quite painful.

Humdrum lives

When I was a kid my lessons at Sunday School were gripping but gruesome. I was not a soulful child, and to pep up my piety and prepare me for life's realities, my teacher told me about slaughtered saints and the good and godly folk, who had refused to abjure their faith and had in consequence been hung, drawn, chopped, and flayed alive. He hoped their example would encourage me and urged me to become a modern Maccabee, but these true but terrible tales of persecutions and pogroms gave me nightmares not zeal. I wet the bed, and my lessons were promptly discontinued. I was sent to the cinema instead.

This was no loss as my lessons did not prove relevant to my later life, which has been unexpectedly safe and suburban. Nobody has asked me to abjure my faith – no one has been that interested either way – and I was also too young for the last war and I shall be too old for the next. My religious education was all about great and grand things, but my life, like that of most people, has consisted of little things.

My greatest problem is so humdrum and small it might seem silly. Like lots of ordinary people, I suffer from stress, worry and mild depression as I face the day. On bad days I can't draw the curtains and the telephone makes me tremble. My problem is not great or grandiose, just laughable, though crippling.

It took me a long time to realise redemption was hidden in little things – too commonplace to be taught by my teachers or noticed in their textbooks. I am saved by boots, brushes and polish. As the leather begins to glow, some hope begins to glow in me.

I am also saved by single socks; I can just manage to match them and when I make a pair I repair my confidence too. I can't cope with serious deeds, but the little kindnesses I give and receive bring back my courage. I make a morning cuppa for my mother. I get a card from a friend in Holland who is a fellow sufferer. He always seems to know the right time to write. Small stuff, but it makes all the difference in a depression.

When I'm down, I don't bellow out brave blessings. I squeak out 'All Things Bright and Beautiful' instead, in a shaky voice, and it works – the world seems a bit brighter.

Only God can know what is big and small in a human life, what is heroic or humdrum, what unnoticed bravery is required by ordinary people trying to do ordinary things in their ordinary lives.

Little things can mean a lot, like these little Jewish light-bulb jokes which lighten my mornings with a little laughter. They might lighten yours too.

How many Jewish fools do you need to change a light bulb? Three! One to hold the bulb in and two to turn the chair he's standing on.

How many Jewish hippies are needed to change a light bulb? Two! One to change the bulb, and one to share the experience. But does the light bulb want to change?

How many Yiddisher mommas are needed to change a light bulb? None! 'Who cares? So we'll all sit in the dark!'

You can enjoy yourself by working out gentile variations. How many bishops does it take to change a light bulb? Over to you . . .

A guru hunt

Many years ago, when I was still at school, I decided there must be somebody who had the answers to life's problems and being a conscientious youngster I decided to find him. I went to the public library, the reference section, and after explaining myself to the librarian was given copies of classy weeklies (such as *Times and Tide*, the *Spectator*, the *New Statesman and Nation*). I skipped the articles because the writers never stopped talking about each other, and as I had never heard of any of them they didn't make much sense.

I found what I wanted in the adverts and heaved a sigh of relief, for gurus were not, as I had feared, in short supply like everything else at that time. All I had to do was make the rounds, find the right one, and then sink back in blissful undisturbed belief.

Armed with a tube of lozenges, I haunted Conway Hall, where I learned that religion was dead. I then trotted off to a church down the road where I was told that humanism had had it. I waited patiently in an anarchist coffee bar, and consumed cups of lukewarm tea in draughty mission halls. I learned the seeker's facts of life: gurus gave you biscuits but wanted a donation; revolutionaries only gave you bits, sometimes, but they were free. I was adjured not to wear a tie as it was bourgeois, and I put mine away with regret. It had been given to me by an uncle from America and had red roses on blue satin whorls and I was very fond of it. But if art had to be renounced for the cause, so be it. I also remember being told that 'the moon feeds a human life'. I could make nothing of this, then or since, but it has stuck in my mind like a lot of other strange information, such as advice about planting parsnips under the full moon.

I never found anyone with The Answer but en route I learned a lot about myself and others, and I am grateful to London's intellectual underworld because it gave me as good an education as the universities I later attended, and was also a lot cheaper and more fun.

I learned, for example, that completely genuine people were rare. But this did not make me bitter, because I also found out that completely phoney people were rare also. Most people, I began to realise, were a mixture of the two – genuine phoneys, in fact. I then found out what was even more important: that I was like most people. I don't know any other way I could have learned this so soon.

I learned also the art of ideological self-protection. Lots of people want to take a trip to heaven – many get taken for a ride. At some point in those draughty halls, I decided I wasn't going to be cannon-fodder for any leader in search of an empire.

In addition, I learned something very important about teachers. I found out that everyone, not just the people on the platform, had a little bit of the truth, and though it wasn't possible to find The Teacher who had it all, if you put all the bits of truth together and added your own bit of truth, you had a composite guru. That's not a very romantic truth but it's serviceable and democratic.

Later on, young people hitched their way to holy men in the Himalayas. Some suffered austerities, and some tried to smoke their way to the sublime. Some discovered deep contemplation, some ended up in cloud-cuckoo-land, and some in asylums. Was their journey really necessary? As much as my shorter journeys riding the

152

London buses. We all had to journey through the world outside us, to discover the truths inside us we already possessed.

It's cold outside

Many years ago, when the autumn evenings darkened, I stumbled upon a synagogue in Soho, marooned among the strip clubs. After the evening prayers, an old man passed me on the pavement and pressed sixpence into my hand. 'I'm not a beggar!' I protested indignantly. 'We all need help,' he said and invited me to his attic for a glass of lemon tea.

Years later I learned that I had taken tea with a great mystic, one of the last Cabbalists of London, who could read hearts and seek out signs.

I poured out my problem to him, one which is still with me though less often now, thank God! I sweat with fright, worrying about something small – a form I can't fill in, or a recipe that went wrong, or whether I had caught dry rot from the rafters. It hits me a.m. not p.m., as I've said before. 'Was God punishing me for some secret sin?' I asked him.

'No, no,' he said gently. 'It is not a punishment but a privilege to suffer such things. Perhaps God is taking the worries of the world from someone whose shoulders cannot carry them, and putting them on yours which can. He has chosen you to help Him in His work of redemption.'

Now that's high stuff, but when you too want to dive back under your duvet, here are my tips to help and redeem you from your own fears. They concern prayer and the papers, because they are the only two realities which reach me before I get up.

Use your prayers to build yourself up, not to pull yourself down. Forget your sins for a moment. Perhaps you've brooded over them too much and they've turned sour. Think about your successes instead, the horrors that never happened, the recipes you got right. Concentrate on something you've enjoyed. If you pray for it, God might give you another helping.

If the news depresses you, make up your own. It's equally true. At this moment three million contented Christians are crashing into crispy rashers, thirty thousand jubilant Jews into cherry jam on rye bread, and a million married couples are coupling, to make love not war, before they bound out of bed. Now, isn't that cheering?

And if you too would like to do likewise but can't, because you haven't got the desire or opportunity, don't mope, what about some fried bread instead? It's just as tasty, more economical and will tempt you back to life. So will this Jewish story which is appropriate to your problem, as it mixes some merriment into morning misery.

There was a depressed Jewish guy who was out of luck. His business was bankrupt, his wife had left him, and as a last straw, even the bread he buttered for himself at breakfast fell on the floor. Moodily, he went to pick it up when suddenly he saw it had fallen buttered side up. Was this a sign his luck had changed?

He rushed round to the rabbi. Could he confirm that his luck had changed? His rabbi examined the slice intently and pored over a pile of pious volumes. 'I'm sorry,' he said to the man sadly, 'but I'm afraid it's just a mistake. You buttered the wrong side, that's all.'

Now, what with benedictions, breakfasts and jokes, you've had enough redemption, so up you get. One, two, three. Yes, I know. Baby, it's cold outside!

Becoming a man

The Bar Mitzvah party was drawing to its close. Saturated with piety and pastries, the guests were thanking their hosts and making late farewells. The confirmation had gone off well, and everything that was supposed to be said in the speeches had been said.

The boy had read from the scroll in the synagogue without a single mistake – so his father said. I had spotted three but kept quiet about it.

The rabbi had urged him to be a modern Maccabee and fight the good fight. His father had exhorted him to play the game – and he didn't mean poker, ha ha – and marry a girl with a heart as big as his mother's, which was impossible, of course. The guests had chorused 'hear, hear!' The boy had committed himself, rather recklessly I thought, to a life of unlimited virtue, to abstain from pork and other impurities not to be mentioned. He promised to marry a nice Jewish girl who would love his mother as she deserved, which was impossible, of course.

Exhausted by so many prayers and promises, the Bar Mitzvah boy and I stared at each other over the debris on the table.

'What loot did you get?' I asked.

'Four fountain pens, seven ties, three watches and a video. What did you get at yours?'

'A gas mask, four savings stamps, three clothing coupons and half a packet of dried egg – there was a war on.'

'It couldn't have been much of a party,' he commented.

'It was fabulous,' I said. 'My father went to Epstein the famous sculptor and commissioned him to model my head in chopped egg and onions for the top table.'

'And did he?' asked the boy, round-eyed.

'No,' I said and shook my head sadly. 'He said he only worked in chopped liver, and my father should try Henry Moore instead.'

'Oh, you're just another joker,' said the boy. 'I wish someone would give me some straight answers sometimes,' he added exasperated.

I thought back to my own Bar Mitzvah and all the questions I hadn't dared to ask. 'Go ahead,' I said. 'I'll answer straight.'

'Well, do you believe all the stuff you read in the prayer book?' he asked.

'No,' I said, 'I can't.'

He looked startled. 'Doesn't that worry you?'

'It used to,' I admitted, 'but not now. The prayer book states what our forefathers believed – yours and mine – but my life has been different from theirs. I've had experiences they never had, and if I try to believe exactly the way they did, it wouldn't work. It would feel as strange as wearing their clothes. But when I recite the prayers, I'm loyal. I add my own faith to theirs, and their prayers continue through mine.'

This was a new thought and he asked, 'But you do practise what you preach, don't you?'

'Not even that,' I said gently. 'I try to, like you, but I fall down, say sorry, pick myself up and fall down again. I don't stop trying though. That's why I'm religious. Perfect people don't need religion.'

'It's so complicated,' the boy said fretfully.

'Yes,' I said, 'but you're a man now and you have to cope with the complications. The truth makes you free – it doesn't make you cosy.'

'Is that from scripture?' he said.

'Yes,' I said, 'but not ours, though the rabbis said the same sort of thing. That's another complication.'

He got up and said good-night politely. He had stepped into grown-up religion and wasn't sure if he liked it.

Laughter in the launderette

Many years ago, when I visited America, an elderly theologian asked me if I would like to accompany him to a nightclub which was a College of Striptease, because it was the only college in those parts which had never given him an honorary doctorate. I still don't know whether his invitation was real or a joke because I was too snooty to accept.

Which was a pity, for there are many unofficial colleges where you can learn the lessons of life. In seminaries they teach you how to be a good Christian or a good Jew or whatever, but it was in a launderette I learned something more basic – how to be a helpful human being.

I'm not married, and I haven't got any children. I'm a bit of a misfit in my own religious world, where everybody is playing 'Happy Families' except me. I used to get home after synagogue, light the festival candles for Chanukah while my dog looked on, and then burst into tears of self-pity and loneliness. My congregation were a nice lot, who pressed invitations on me, but if you're the perpetual guest you feel second class and get choked by charity.

I was rescued by my neighbour from the next bedsit but one. He asked me to watch his washing while he went for a bit of curry with his girl. I sat contentedly in the warmth with my dog and a bottle of festival wine, hypnotised by the laundry going round and round. Beside me were secretaries doing their smalls, students staring into the *New Statesman*, one-parent families keeping one eye on single children, and a be-draggled beggar attracted by the steamy warmth on a cold night.

I learned how to fold sheets, share my wine, and match mixed socks. I also learned that there were lots of people like me who were outsiders inside their own society. Perhaps there were more people who didn't fit in than those who did. I also watched God at work, making a family out of us, not through ties of blood but through laundry, and helping each other out. The old extended family of my childhood had gone, but in a big city your new family are your friends, though there is no liturgy that notices it, and no special blessings to sanctify it.

The launderette was a tougher world than I was used to and its humour was blacker. A man stood on a city bridge. 'Keep away all of you,' he shouted, 'I've had enough,' and he jumped off into the water. An onlooker threw off his coat and shoes, and dived in after him. As he swam near, the man shouted again, 'Don't save me, I've made up my mind!'

'I don't want to save you, mate,' said the other, 'I just want to know where you work.'

After that I never cried again in front of the Chanukah candles. My pay and prospects weren't wonderful, but at least I had some security and status and some food to share with my new family, so I blessed God instead.